UN-AGORAPHOBIC

UN-AGORA-PHOBIC

OVERCOME ANXIETY,
PANIC ATTACKS,
AND AGORAPHOBIA
FOR GOOD

A STEP-BY-STEP PLAN

HAL MATHEW

Conari Press

First published in 2014 by Weiser Books
Red Wheel/Weiser, LLC
With offices at:
665 Third Street, Suite 400
San Francisco, CA 94107
www.redwheelweiser.com

Mathew, Hal.
  Un-agoraphobic : overcome anxiety, panic attacks, and agoraphobia for good : a step-by-step plan / Hal Mathew.
      pages cm
  Summary: "A wonderfully comprehensive, step-by-step self-help
program for overcoming agoraphobia and panic attacks"-- Provided by publisher.
  ISBN 978-1-57324-639-2 (paperback)
1. Agoraphobia--Treatment--Popular works. 2. Panic attacks-
-Treatment--Popular works. 3.   Anxiety--Treatment--Popular
works. I. Title.

  RC552.A44M377 2014
  616.85'225--dc23

                                              2014023658

Cover design by Jim Warner
Interior by Jane Hagaman
Typeset in Sabon

Printed in the United States of America.
EBM
10 9   8 7 6 5 4 3 2 1

CONTENTS

To Krissie and to Christy
and to all my pals living with
and working with mental illness

INTRODUCTION

How did you get here, deep in the clutches of this #@!&%*! *curse* known as agoraphobia? Were you born with it? Choose it? Conditioned by your environment? No one seems to be certain what causes panic attacks, or why some people who suffer from panic attacks become agoraphobic. I've developed theories, and you will no doubt develop some more. We know it starts with a panic attack, then turns into panic disorder, which I define as fear of fear, causing avoidance. The avoidance, in turn, becomes agoraphobia. Once you have a couple of panic attacks and the indescribable fear they bring, you live in dread that you might have another, at any moment and with no warning. This keeps you on edge and, therefore, more likely to have another panic attack. It's a cruel, consuming cycle.

Let's get down to basics. You want your life back. Life. You can't get any more basic than that. How much longer are you going to let this panic creature rule? Why does it get to constrain your life, your essence, your days and nights, in a dark dungeon of despair? Isn't it about time for *you* to rule? You *can* free yourself from your prison. You can, and you *will!* Here's where we cue the cheers and wild applause. Go ahead, bask in it.

How do I know you can do this? Because I did.

What's more, there really are no big mysteries you need to crack, or secrets you need to know, to free yourself. Your cure will come from persistent hard work, creative thinking, and a loving change of attitude about your misdirected fear-response system, all under the careful (and sometimes zany) guidance of the book you are holding right now. The book says hello, by the way, it's a pleasure to meet you.

Your First Kiss (of Death)

What was your first one like? Most people who end up agoraphobic can recall vivid details from the first time the train ran over them. Life is so palpable, so vibrant, so intense at the onset of a panic attack that the experience is seared into your brain as if with a red-hot branding iron. This is one of life's crueler realizations: you suddenly discover that your body came equipped with a kick-ass, state-of-the-art alarm system, but you can't find any instructions on how to turn the screeching thing off.

You find yourself in the middle of some sort of blast zone. You are acutely aware, but you're not sure of what. The not knowing makes the experience even more frightening.

In a matter of seconds, you went from being a normal person having a normal day to becoming the most desperate creature on the planet. You don't know what's happening to you, and you certainly don't know what to do about it. How or why the emergency started is a mystery. The thought slams into your brain: *Run! But where?* The thought of running makes you more scared. You need a safe place *now!* This is quickly getting out of hand. You can't control your thoughts, and you can't even draw a full breath. You look around for something or someone to save you, but everything is foreign and unfamiliar. The whole world seems chaotic and threatening, and you are far from any safe place.

You don't dare start screaming. Do you? Your limbs tremble as you move about with increasing urgency, but there is still no help anywhere in sight. Your hands are tingling and shaking, and sweat gathers on your face. Your terrible dilemma seems to be worsening by the second. Frantic, you consider desperate measures like injuring yourself and calling for an ambulance so you can get to a hospital and be anesthetized. *Help!!!*

That one blood-curdling experience led to another, and another, which led to your present status of being constantly in fear. Who wouldn't be afraid of a monster that leaps out in front of you without warning, sinks its teeth and claws into your flesh, and viciously shakes your body and soul until you're afraid you will die, and then slinks off to its sulfurous hiding place, leaving you in a frightened and battered heap, afraid you might *not* die? Who wouldn't be afraid of that?

This sucks. All you know for certain is you never, ever want to have one of those again. From now on, each time you venture out, you have to be constantly alert to this gruesome new threat. You begin to avoid places or circumstances that might cause another panic attack, but the attacks persist. You continue to eliminate possible triggers, and finally there are places you can no longer go and things you can no longer do.

Anxiety is constant, like a heavy, scratchy overcoat you can't remove. You're such a good person, you intone, why should you be a helpless victim of whatever this is? You hate to go to bed because, first, you can't sleep and, second, there's the horrifying prospect of waking up terrified at three a.m. with no help, madly trying to think of someone you can call. And then you hate to wake up in the morning because you are instantly jangled by the noise and demands of the chaotic world.

Once you're up, you fixate on developing strategies to somehow keep yourself together for another day without having a you-know-what. You try to eat breakfast while reading the paper (aka *The Daily Struggle*), but everything you read and hear seems jarring and your throat closes so tightly that swallowing is difficult.

What now?

So here we are. Your automatic fear-response system is now on overload, hyperdrive, totally malfunctioning. And it's all your fault. Why? Through only the best intentions—trying to protect yourself from another attack—you have given the fear-response apparatus in your brain too many jobs to do, too many things to be on alert for. Meet your amygdala: the decision-making center of the brain, the on switch for floods of adrenaline coursing through your panicked veins.[1] Your amygdala is on high alert. Left unchecked, it has lumped any possible trigger or fear-

Un-Agoraphobic

ful sensation into one big pile. And the sign near the pile says *Extreme Danger.* The amygdala is an integral part of the brain; without it we wouldn't survive because we wouldn't have anything to alert us to (truly) extreme danger. But puhlease! There seems to be some misunderstanding here about what constitutes extreme danger. A flickering fluorescent light?! A long bridge??!! A *thought!!?* You and your amygdala need to talk.

I've got a plan. What we'll be doing together in this book, day by day and step by step, is replacing the long-established patterns of reaction to stimuli that give you endless anxiety-filled days and panic attacks. We will do this by systematically creating regular patterns of thought and activity that will lay the foundations for new neural pathways of positive thinking. In short, you are going to *change your mind.*

I think we get frightened and take flight so readily because we're still hardwired to deal with continual physically dangerous encounters in the way our ancient ancestors were.[2] Never mind that the likelihood of being in a life-threatening situation when you venture out your front door has diminished greatly over the past several thousand years. I'm thinking perhaps we don't *need* a five-gallon tank of epinephrine (a fancy word for adrenaline). In this era of the occasional mugging or carjacking, the rare bomb, perhaps a quart would do the trick. And maybe the trigger doesn't have to be *quite* so autocratic. It would be nice if we could vote on whether or not a particular incident was worth wasting two or three gallons of adrenaline (and ruining the week).

I wonder if the Evolution Committee is working on that yet. (The EC is an imaginary group that meets in my mind whenever I observe a need for progress in humanoid skill levels.) Hmmm. Maybe I can put in a request to speed up, you know, evolution. Probably only need to make some minor genetic modifications to the triggering mechanism in order to provide a cure to millions of cheering agoraphobia sufferers, after all. But I'm wandering now. Until the Evolution Committee makes some changes, the human alarm system will continue to be ridiculously overpowered, making all "threats" feel real to especially sensitive people like you. After all, that's its job. In that flash of lightning when the adrenaline button is punched, nearly every organ in your body is brought to the fight. But the good news is, you can stop the fight. You're writing the script of your own life, so you can turn a tense, dramatic moment into a light one at a moment's notice.

Three Levels

Through my own experience and in countless support groups and counseling sessions, I have created three levels of agoraphobia to distinguish between various phases of anxiety. Most of us experience each of the three at one time or another.

> **Level 1**—Housebound, or mostly so
>
> **Level 2**—Partially mobile
>
> **Level 3**—Mobile, with a wall

When you are at Level 1, you may actually be experiencing less noticeable anxiety than when you are at Level 2, but life in a cell is still miserable. What's worse, sometimes even being inside your home doesn't feel safe enough and you have to be inside a small space inside your home. I once spent an entire Saturday in my shower stall, desperately and thoroughly scrubbing tiles until my wife came home from work. The best you can do at Level 1 is occasionally venture out the door, some days down to the end of the block, where you wave merrily at the postal person, the only live human you might see that day.

This is not what you wanted to be doing with your life. Being homebound is probably easier with all the electronic distractions available, but you can't escape feeling that, while being inside is saving you, it is also killing you, killing you softly. I did one of my homebound spells with soap operas on black-and-white TV. To this day, I can't look at a soap opera.

When you are at Level 2, you can usually get to your job or school or whatever outside obligation you have, but it never gets easy. Once you are out the door, the world is a hostile place. You sweat and gasp for air as you make your way to your destination. If you are lucky, your daytime gig is comfortable and feels reasonably safe. Oddly, people at Level 2 can make excellent students or employees because we totally focus on the task at hand in order to shut out unwanted thoughts. A high-pressure job can be just the ticket for someone at Level 2 who needs to be busy every second. (I was never much of a student, but I got almost straight A's during my anxiety-ridden year and a half of graduate school to escape the military draft.)

If you also experience high anxiety at work, though, the trip home can be a nightmare. What if you get stuck in traffic or your transportation breaks down or a long train blocks a crossing? In the winter, those long, long lines of streetlights quicken your heart rate. You display your talent for catastrophic thinking. If you are lucky, you can finally feel relief when you get home. On the other hand, you may be coming home to stressful family demands that overwhelm you. When you have people depending on you, there is just no break from anxiety. Or, being home, especially on weekends, can be hard because you feel isolated and miss your weekday contacts. At any rate, your life at Level 2 is going downhill and you keep asking yourself, *What's the point?* You are seeking desperately for answers, but you don't know what questions to ask.

The time in Level 3 can be easy time indeed. This is the cycle when daily anxiety almost disappears and you haven't had a panic attack in a while. You often wake up without that familiar sense of dread and can meet most of your daily obligations without feeling fearful. You might even go to a movie (aisle seat toward the back) or for a stroll in the mall (at a slow time with the car parked near an exit you noted carefully on the way in). You can smile, you can laugh, you can have a successful relationship. Life at Level 3 can be too easy, however, and make you complacent. You have to keep remembering that although there are lots of things you can do, there's still that one

Un-Agoraphobic

very big thing you can't—an invisible line you can't imagine being able to cross.

Life at Level 3 can be heartbreaking because you're so near yet so far from being able to travel freely. Every weekend, you watch your friends and neighbors tossing their backpacks and suitcases into vehicles, leaving you behind as they venture beyond the Great Wall that imprisons you. In a small enough town, you might be the only one left to guard the water supply on the Fourth of July.

You get very good at making excuses and inventing stories to keep spouses, children, parents, bosses, and friends off your back. The bad news is, you know from history that the beast can leap out and tear you to pieces again at any moment. You are not feeling fulfilled. This is not a wonderful life, but the good news is, you are at the perfect place to begin your Recovery Program. This is exciting—I feel like you're a long-lost relative who has a fabulous inheritance you didn't know was coming: freedom.

Life can be unfair, as many people know. It seems very unfair that so many people have been blindsided by agoraphobia. Fortunately, this huge, horrible, hairy, scary thing that climbs tall buildings and wreaks havoc on so many lives is simply—dare I say it?—imaginary. You knew that, of course, but the built-in fear-response system we all possess sure makes whatever is causing the panic attack seem like a real *something*. There are certainly real emotional and physical conditions that result from this something, whatever it is.

No matter where you are with your panic attacks and your restrictions, I've been there. I ran the gamut more than once during my thirty years as a prisoner of agoraphobia—from housebound to county line-bound, from desperate to determined. I succumbed to it, and I fought it. I lost ground, and I gained ground, and I repeated the patterns time and again. Finally, I learned to stop struggling and turned to healing. I realized I had to become whole again before I could become free again.

Had I known how to create a holistic approach to surviving and overcoming panic attacks early in the game, and how I could have benefited from specific brain activities, I would have recovered much sooner of course. I'm happy to be able to give you a way to benefit from all I learned. I recall feeling mostly *lost* and *disconnected* during those early years, suffering the anxiety of isolation because I did not know how to explain my secret fears to anyone, nor how to get help. As I learned more about myself and my mental problem, though, and discovered there were other people like me, I began to feel the security of being a part of something, and my fears diminished somewhat. It almost felt like safety in numbers when I began making connections via books and magazines to significant therapists, to writers and scientists, and later, to peer support group members.

How It Started

Before we begin to build your personal recovery program, I'd like to reveal to you where my ideas about recovery originated and how and why I wrote a book for you based on what I learned and created during my forty years living with the panic disorder creature.

It began on a dark and stormy night when I burst out the front door of my family's apartment while I was babysitting my brother and ran, screaming, down the snow-covered street, barefoot in my pajamas with *something* coming after me. The worst feeling I'd had up to that point in my young life was when I'd lost my best marble, a boulder clearie, in a schoolyard match. That was a bummer, but suddenly I was hysterically running for my life on a dark winter night from a monster I could not see but could certainly feel.

I was experiencing the most primal of human responses—Full Force Fear. There was no apparent stimulus—nothing there to be afraid of—but my hair-trigger fight-or-flight system had just gone off, blasting into my nervous system a highly charged cocktail of hormones designed to momentarily turn an ordinary human into a primitive beast so suddenly strong and single-minded that it can kill or seriously harm a foe. There are documented, witnessed instances of ordinary people lifting cars off people while in a full adrenaline fury.[3]

I was only ten years old, and the rage and fear boiling inside from a sudden infusion of monster juice created a feeling of terror so extreme I didn't think I'd live through it. All I could do was run for my life.

But I don't have to tell you.

They call them "panic attacks," which I'm sure we'll all agree is a pale and inadequate phrase for something that can change your life forever. That one horror movie did change my life forever (just as your first panic attack experience changed you). During the next forty years, I would adapt and create and struggle; I would make some gains and then fall back into the hole and start climbing out again. I learned a lot. I tried one thing and then another, building a supply of techniques and tricks that helped in little ways and big ways to steer me toward recovery as well as survive each grueling day.

A young kid has to grow up in a hurry when something frightening and mysterious happens. Seeing no apparent solutions to my problem, I had to start thinking about life as a difficult challenge. The woman down the street who came running out to catch me was able to allay my immediate fears by taking me in, wrapping me with a blanket, giving me cocoa, and calling my grandparents, who located my parents. I can still recall the puzzled and anxious expressions as the four of them pushed into the woman's small living room, inquiring what had happened to me. That's what *I* wanted to know.

Consoling words and hugs can't take away the kind of deep-seated fear that sets in after a panic attack, especially the very first one. No one around me, even in the medical community, seemed to understand what I was going through. I certainly couldn't explain. It seemed I had been afflicted with some sort of craziness, even though the family matriarch, Aunt Eunice, said, "If you think you're crazy, you're not." I'm sure that was a relief to everyone else.

By the end of the school year, I was feeling okay again and had pretty much returned to my usual childhood happiness. Until two years later . . . it happened again on a hunting trip with my father and his boss—two macho men whom I didn't feel like I could ask for help. Not that I even knew what to ask for. The trip was an unending nightmare and left me feeling anxious that whole year in school, seventh grade, during which time I had a few more panic attacks. The two-year pattern continued, with several month-long periods of intense anxiety followed by a return to feeling fairly normal. I had a cluster of panic attacks when I was fourteen and again at sixteen. Then, about two years later came *the bomb*.

It happened just after my nineteenth birthday, when I was a college sophomore in a car with other young student actors touring central Montana with a couple of Robert Frost plays. My life was going very well; I had no stressors I can recall. We did a performance in one small town, stayed over, and the next day were driving north through some hilly timbered country when we came out of a narrow canyon and emerged onto the land of never-ending openness—the Montana plains. They go on forever, flat and drab and suffocatingly frightening to a person like me. Those claiming normalcy would view the same wide open spaces with probable boredom. Why the difference? We don't know, but the panic attack I had on the spot (and managed to conceal from my friends) was so scary that it prevented me from traveling freely again for another thirty years. The rest of that trip was even worse than the hunting trip at age twelve. From that point on, I felt a large black *A* for *agoraphobe* was branded into my forehead.

I managed to graduate college and get married and get a good job despite all, but it was a bloody struggle most of the way, some of which you'll read about in the book. That was then, and this is now.

The most important thing now is *you*. You need help, and I'm glad you asked (by buying this book). I've been out of prison more than twenty years. I'm your guy.

Listen to Your Brain

What you are looking for *immediately* is some way to stop being so tense all the time and so petrified of panic attacks. You want to be able to sit down, put your feet up, and totally relax as you once did. What's stopping you? You're afraid if you let up your guard even for an instant, a major panic attack will take hold of you and turn you every which way but loose.

Well, you know something? Your brain has a lot of good ideas if you would just listen.

Notice I've said *your brain,* not *your mind*.[4] Your mind, by my definition, is what you've made so far with the Big Machine you were given. Because your mind is made up of not only what was already in the brain but also of stuff you've been bringing in and storing, things can go awry. If you overload yourself with bad data, your mind may turn into a big mess from time to time. But your brain won't.

Here's what the Brain will tell you if you ask honestly and listen honestly: "I am smart enough and strong enough to take care of any and all emergencies. We don't have to look outside for help when panic looms; look inside. You are all you need in this particular emergency—a panic attack—so rely on yourself. Let's turn off the adrenaline machine and look objectively at what's going on here."

That's what your brain will tell you if you pay attention. Pose the question this way: *Listen, Brain, I need some information from you, see, and I need it fast. Are you smart enough and strong enough to overcome agoraphobia, and can you start right away?*

You won't have to wait long for the answer. That brain always thinks it's smarter than us (ever noticed its little voice that's forever saying, "I knew it was a bad idea—didn't I tell you that was a bad idea?" or, "I could have told you that"?). I ask you, what ego-driven brain will say it's not smart enough or strong enough to do *anything?* Brains are like men in that way. They will say they can do something when there's no apparent evidence that they can. In this case, trust it. When your brain settles on the task, don't let your mind get in its way. Your brain can do this work very well if you give it the job and train it well.

In the meantime, you're probably going to be inclined to do everything you can to physically hold on to your sanity. You will feel like you need to be constantly vigilant. That, as you will soon learn, is the opposite of what you need to be. You are going to be unbelievably happy to no longer have heavy anxiety clinging to you all day, every day. Change is coming, and it's going to feel great.

Here's something to chew on, agoraphobes: your overreactions to a given stimulus are simply products of a physiological response that you can change. Let me say that last part again: *that you can change*. The amazing area of brain study called "neuroplasticity" has lots of good news for you in terms of replacing the automatic triggers that are now betraying you. Neuroscientists have proven that new neural pathways can be created throughout the nervous system, including in the brain, by employing regular thought patterns and activities.

The fact is, if you start doing a lot of thinking about a particular matter, your brain will actually change physiologically as new neural pathways are hooked up in the direction of your thoughts. I'm oversimplifying it, but you'll be learning more as we go (see chapter 4, "Change Your Own Mind: Positive Thinking and Visualization").

Why would anyone ever use all those badly programmed, misleading thought pathways that are constantly leading to despair? Prepare to totally rethink the *problem* so you can write the solution and completely reverse some of your body's automatic ways of responding. But wait! There's more. This book also helps you regain the confidence and courage you need as well as teach you how to create and discover the right tools to use for your own personal victory. Each person's solution is different, but all solutions start with good ideas.

This book provides you with specific assignments and work activities, all designed to give you structure in your day and help the *whole* you recover. Not until I finally put in place the last pieces of my puzzle could I see the whole picture *and* the disorder. This approach enables me to line up all the pieces for you from the start and give you everything you need to solve your own puzzle and create your own path to freedom. You will learn how to make the inward and outward connections that will bring you *peace* and *wisdom:* the ultimate antidotes to anxiety and agoraphobia.

What's more, I know you are going to enjoy doing all the work I've set up for you, especially if you do it from your heart. Your gladdened heart will lead the way to an amazing future, making it easier for you to look in the mirror each morning and say those three little words. Self-love is vital to your recovery, and by picking up this book and beginning this program, you've already shown that you know about the love-recovery connection. Here you are, after all, taking care of yourself.

Beyond this book, there are unlimited resources available to you online and through your local bookstore and library. You will be able to begin working on your recovery program straightaway. The immediate reward will be this: you will start to feel more in control and confident as soon as you start working. The work you do today will very quickly lead to reduced stress because you will feel relieved that you've finally begun a series of positive steps to heal yourself. Reduced stress will lead to easier breathing, easier breathing will lead to happier thoughts, and on and on. Life will keep getting easier.

The result of this work is that you will stop fearing panic attacks and never have another. You will be free. What's more, you'll be able to reach back and help another agoraphobe who's feeling hopeless.

The solution is surprisingly simple, but not exactly easy to arrive at. Don't get me wrong—you're in a fine mess, and it will take plenty of hard work to get out of it. But you have a plan (this book) and hope. There is no doubt you will succeed if you work at it.

By using this book and faithfully doing the work, you will begin to notice a change in your emotions— probably in just a few days. You will find that your mind is more alert and charged up, as you consciously and subconsciously start thinking about change and recovery. Do not misinterpret these emotions. This heightened sensation is not your daily anxiety; it's more like *excitement*.

Remain positive and the new stirrings will give you the boost you need to throw yourself into this and do the recovery work. It's good to be and *feel* excited. And it's safe. Once you get the ball rolling and do creative work (nearly) every day, you won't be able to stop the ball from rolling until you are completely and forever free of panic disorder and everything that comes with it. You are going to be free, my friend. Totally.

Once you start working on this program, you will find that you are almost unknowingly creating subtle changes in your ways of thinking, day after day, as your new neural pathways take hold. As you're on the recovery path, you will have major victories from time to time, such as being able to drive to work again. However, most of the changes will occur quietly as you're doing such daily tasks as research and writing in your journal. The changes will be prompted by thoughts that seep in but don't necessarily create dramatic (or even noticeable) changes at the time. What I'm saying is, carry on even if you're not noticing continuous or dramatic improvement. It's there.

You will be creating your own Recovery Program, because recovery is a highly personal thing. We each need to figure out which tactics and words and ideas to develop in order to bring about an entire change in the way we think about the deep mysterious fear that has been ruling us. By studying fear, writing about fear, and talking about fear, you learn day by day what you specifically need to do to regain control of your life.

This book helps you get to know who you are and the amazing things you're capable of accomplishing. Once you understand and accept your exceptional abilities, things will be easier. This book starts with some basic questions and answers about what we're working with here, and then it dives into a structured daily work plan. The daily work program in *Un-agoraphobic* is designed to help you make discoveries—many every day—that will help you realize a new way to think about and/or take control of everyday problems you couldn't manage as recently as last week.

There are specific things you can start doing today to begin that process. I don't mean today as some abstract notion; I mean *today*. Look at the calendar. What day is it? Get up and circle it because this is the day you will begin the turnaround. Here's what I want you to do before bed tonight, to make the first night of your new life productive as well as fun. I want you to tell yourself a story that begins thusly:

Once upon a time, there was a sad young/middle-aged/old prince/princess (that's you!) who had been imprisoned in a tower overlooking a beautiful land filled with happy, industrious people who came and went as they pleased. This prisoner was unable to join those people because of a terrible case of mistaken identity. You see, an evil princess/prince had committed unforgivable crimes against the people, but it was you, the lookalike cousin, who got arrested and tried for those crimes, and punished in the cruelest of ways.

Despite your pleas of innocence, the courts ordered that a chip be implanted in your brain that created constant feelings of fear, anxiety, and panic attacks. You were then placed in the tower whose only lock was your fear, more than enough to prevent you from roaming about your kingdom. Through the small barred window, you could sometimes be heard crying out, "Could I please have the fifty daily lashes instead?"

A long time passed, and you gave up hope. One day an elderly, retired Interpol inspector named Clousseau was puttering around the office, being helpful by putting away old wanted posters, when he came across the one showing the evil princess/prince, whom he recalled the whole country had been looking for at one time. As he looked closer, he suddenly realized he lived right across the street

Un-Agoraphobic

from the person in the wanted poster. He went straight into the chief inspector's office (without knocking) and said those famous words: "Chief Inspector, the wrong person is in the tower prison."

So here we are! Tomorrow is the day the specialist comes to remove the anxiety chip from your brain. (Don't worry, it's outpatient surgery with a local anesthetic. Nothing major.) The reparation program will allow you total freedom to create an entire new life at the state's expense.

Go to bed a little early tonight, and as you're drifting into sleep, start creating your new life.

Enjoy inventing ways to make going to sleep a positive and useful experience every night. This will prepare you for visualization work you'll be doing later.

I know this will work, but I have to remind you that there is no applicable time frame here. There just isn't. As I reflect on my recovery, I don't think I would have trusted something that happened quickly. Did I mention it's a good idea to be patient? I know I would have felt more comfortable being patient if I'd *known* for certain, as you do, that total recovery was possible.

One day you will notice you no longer fear a particular thing; another day you'll notice you just did something that had once been impossible and you did it without a thought. As the changes build, you will one day wake up and just *know*. On that day, the winds will be favorable, and you will feel strong and confident. That is the day your ship will sail, the day you will be transformed. Or at least you will be emotionally ready to sail, to take your Very Big Trip, even if your actual departure time is briefly delayed by outside circumstances such as work. You will be ready to *go*.

Shall we start?

UNDERSTANDING AGORAPHOBIA 101
QUESTIONS AND ANSWERS

No doubt, if you suffer from agoraphobia yourself, you will know many of these answers already. But I've included some questions and answers here so that we can be on the same page about some basic definitions and assumptions. This section can also be used as a handy information guide for anyone in your life who might benefit from more information about the concepts in this book and about what you are facing as you begin your recovery program.

1. What Is Agoraphobia?

Agoraphobia (Greek for "fear of the marketplace") is an avoidant behavior brought on by repeated panic attacks in circumstances where getting to safety is not immediate or easy—a crowded marketplace or a distant location, for example. (See question 4 for more on panic attacks.) Symptoms of agoraphobia include constant anxiety, panic attacks, fear of traveling beyond a safe area, restlessness and sleeplessness, inability to concentrate, and more. Essentially, agoraphobia is the result, and panic disorder is the cause.

2. What Is Panic Disorder?

Panic disorder by my definition is the general state of anxiousness resulting from having had one too many panic attacks. A person with panic disorder becomes subconsciously alert to the threat of yet another panic, and that gives the sufferer a feeling of constant unease and fearfulness. The result is *fear of fear*.

3. Does This Mean the Person Is "Crazy?"

Panic attacks with agoraphobia is listed as a seriously disabling mental illness in the bible for mental health professionals—*The Diagnostic and Statistical Manual of Mental Disorders*, or *DSM-5* for short. A person who cannot work because of severe agoraphobia qualifies for Social Security disability income. Therefore, if being mentally ill is "crazy," the answer is yes, but it is better to use specific terms for mental illnesses so that everyone knows what you are talking about. In my opinion, *crazy* is a wonderful but much overused word best employed to describe those we can't *prove* are mentally ill but obviously are. As an example, I define the truly crazy people as those who allow themselves to be taken over by a system of capitalism and greed.

Unlike most of the other significant mental illnesses, agoraphobia can be completely cured (witness *moi*). Recovery is easier if treatment starts soon after symptoms appear. Treatment can include self-help (e.g., this book), professional therapy, and short-term use of medication. Agoraphobia should be considered a temporary condition, duration unknown.

4. How Does Somebody Become Agoraphobic?

A person with a history of random panic attacks can develop a heightened sense of alert we call anxiety. Someone constantly on high alert is said to have panic disorder and is almost certain to begin avoiding certain places or circumstances. If avoidance extends to more than one thing or place, agoraphobia is the verdict. Agoraphobia has several levels, from being housebound (Level 1) to being capable of everything but long-distance travel (Level 3). Essentially, it is avoidance of pretty much everything outside a safe circumference. Agoraphobic folks bond with one another easily because they are so much alike; they are as alike as first cousins, if not sisters and brothers.

5. What Causes Panic Attacks?

There is no clear answer to what causes panic attacks, but theories abound. When we are startled or alarmed by something that turns out *not* to be dangerous, our ancestor-tainted fight-or-flight response system can be misled into believing there is a full-scale emergency. As a result, adrenaline floods through our system and blood flows to the muscles, making the body ready for action when there is no action to be had. Pulse, breathing rate, and blood pressure rise for naught. The overwhelming feeling of fear is real, but there is nothing real to fear. This constitutes a panic attack. It seems clear that some people have an elevated susceptibility to being startled and therefore could be the type to unwittingly throw gasoline on the tiny spark of something as harmless as a sudden noise. I surmise that both learned behavior and genetic brain chemistry are involved in making one person likely to easily recover from being startled and another person more easily misled and unable to halt the fight-or-flight response to a mere startle.

Think of an occasion when you were surprised or startled by something that caused you to either freeze or quickly move out of the way. The *something* could have been as harmless to most people as a honeybee, or it could have been an ax-wielding maniac. If the bee wandered off in another direction and disappeared, a "normal" person would return to normal. If the ax maniac persisted, a "normal" person would continue evading or fighting back with the elevated strength and speed provided by a flood of adrenaline. Someone with panic disorder does not know how to turn off the false alarm process once it gets going and must endure a terrifying experience of unknown duration, even if there is nothing apparent to fear. The bee left, but they still got stung.

Neuroscience tells us that two smallish parts of the brain—the amygdala and the hippocampus—are essentially the guards at the gate, taking in all data as it arrives at us.[5] To paraphrase what I have learned from many sources: genetics are involved in determining how we act or react under a given circumstance, but some of the decisions on how to evaluate a given bit of information are made through a deliberate, conscious process. You have, many times in your life, told your brain to go on alert when certain specific things are present because you regard them as dangerous. Our early ancestors had to be on high alert whenever they were away from camp because there were many ferocious critters roaming the earth. The fight-or-flight system allowed a Neanderthal adult to be in full sprint within milliseconds of having seen the fangs of a nearby people eater. But that was then and this is now, so one would think time plus reality would have toned down our defense system a bit.

The truth is, unfortunately, some people have alarm systems that need to be reprogrammed. We all take in squintillions of units of information daily; nearly every time you turn your head, you see changes. Our brains have to filter data so that we can conduct somewhat rational lives without being overwhelmed. The aforementioned amygdala and hippocampus team up to provide our data filter. Try to imagine how many mixed messages have been transmitted from one part of your brain to another and back when things once scary or misinterpreted changed status a few times from scary to friendly to indifferent and back again— something as simple as a particular person at school, for example. Multiply that example by millions of experiences and changes in perception, and we wonder how we ever learn to be afraid of the appropriate things and make the correct response to any given stimuli.

It's not hard for me to understand how a child who is nervous (by nature or circumstance) could be subconsciously telling the information-sorting part of her brain to fear many more sorts of things than a less nervous child might fear. I've spoken to several agoraphobic people who reported troublesome anxiety as youngsters, and my own story is no different. The more things a child decides to fear—and it really is a decision—the more likely the child is to end up in a situation that creates a fearful response.

6. How Do You Cure It?

This book, *Un-agoraphobic*, gives you (or your friend or partner) all the tools needed for full recovery, including information and advice on therapy and medication. I have developed a process for "tricking the mind" and for making the necessary holistic changes in order to fully recover. The agoraphobic person will recover by tricking herself into not fearing panic attacks. Once she stops fearing panic attacks, she will never have another. My advice to an agoraphobic person who wants to recover is to thoroughly read and *do* this book, and throw everything you have into the process.

Briefly, an agoraphobic person needs to do heavy lifting in the following areas: willingness to change, letting go, communication skills, confidence, self-respect, self-knowledge, self-love, knowledge about agoraphobia, and courage. The book demonstrates how to remember joy, how to become calm, how to learn, and how to change. Central to overcoming agoraphobia is the Recovery Program as it is laid out in the book. The program evolves and develops day by day through specific activities and journal writing. Recovery requires diligent work, creative actions, and self-learned tactics. I designed this recovery process so that readers heal from within; rather than follow a strict regimen from me that will heal from the outside, readers instead finally invent a way—their own way—to break out of prison from the inside.

A therapist who specializes in panic and anxiety disorder can greatly assist recovery, and there are some medications that can help if used prudently. There are many ways to offset the costs of these therapies (for more on this, see chapter 7, "Call in the Pros: Therapeutic and Legal Help").

7. Is PTSD Different from Agoraphobia?

Post-traumatic stress disorder is a condition created by severe trauma that causes feelings of extreme fearfulness. When the fear forces the victim into a restricted area, the effect is nearly identical to agoraphobia brought on by panic disorder. There are other paths to agoraphobia, which I'll explain briefly.

Whether it's a single event like a catastrophe or an ongoing stressor like abuse, these kinds of traumas can create PTSD. Unfortunately, a significant number of military people suffer tremendous mental torture because of their experiences in warzones. PTSD causes many of them to isolate and avoid. The condition of agoraphobia can also be the result of a terrible physical illness or health condition. Most sufferers of PTSD require therapy to help them work their way through the emotional effects of the traumatic event or illness.

There are two other anxiety disorders that can cause one to limit mobility. Obsessive compulsive disorder results in avoidance of feared things, limiting the sufferer to certain territories. People suffering from social anxiety disorder can become nearly homebound in worst cases in trying to avoid intimacy.

Some people develop phobic avoidant behaviors because of emetophobia, fear of vomiting, especially in public. Other people have been shown to be prisoners of a certain territory because of falsely held beliefs.

There is another route to panic attacks with the tongue-twitching name of labyrinthitis. A search of Harvard Medical School's website for psychiatric studies revealed a strong correlation between people who develop the inner ear infection called "labyrinthitis" and anxiety leading to panic attacks. Briefly, the researchers noted a similarity between the neural signal associated with labyrinthitis and the neural signals alerting a person to extreme danger. They noted that both the onset of a panic attack and an attack of labyrinthitis, which can cause extreme vertigo, happen instantaneously and without warning. I can confirm that personally. They theorize that the correlation between labyrinthitis and panic attacks is the similarity of the triggers—they appear so much the same that the amygdala might misread the inner ear signals and put out a call to action (panic attack).

Interestingly, I was plagued by labyrinthitis attacks at about the same time I had my first panic attack at age ten. There was no apparent correlation between the two, though. I did not experience a panic attack the few times I had sudden attacks of what is also called "vestibular dysfunction," nor was I suffering inner ear infection symptoms on any of the occasions I had panic attacks. When the inner ear thing happened, I would become instantly so dizzy I couldn't stand; everything whirled around me. Other symptoms were light sensitivity, nausea, and a nasty sinus-like headache. The only thing that seemed to help was to lie in a dark room with a cool washcloth on my forehead. Later I figured out that Dramamine and antihistamines relieved the dizziness symptoms. I had my last attack of labyrinthitis when I was nineteen, the same year I became agoraphobic. I don't really know what to make of any of that; the result was still the same—agoraphobia.

There are a number of websites regarding "labyrinthitis and anxiety," and reading the postings indicates the phenomena is fairly common amongst vertigo sufferers. The reason I never suffered panic attacks when I had vertigo was because the dizziness was sudden and extreme (my theory). If, however, the symptoms had come on more slowly, perhaps I would have misinterpreted and had a panic attack. Since I never had a co-occurrence, the good news for those of you who have panic with vertigo, is that through this book you can overcome your panic disorder and then only (ha!) have to deal with the dizziness and nausea and headaches. Or maybe not. One posting was from a woman who said her vertigo diminished as her mental health improved.

If you have panic disorder and ever had or are suffering from labyrinthitis, please send an email to our website—unagoraphobic@gmail.com—describing your experience. If we get enough people with these cross diagnoses, we can send our anecdotal information on to Harvard Medical's psychiatry department. I'm sure every little bit helps as the medical community strives to provide better care for our particular mental illness.

This book is of help to you on several levels no matter the cause of your avoidant behaviors. *Un-agoraphobic* is a program designed to heal and perfect the whole you when the whole you is shattered by terrifying feelings. Use this book and journal writing to accompany therapy you are or will be undergoing to resolve the trauma that got you to this point in your life. I am deeply sorry you had to experience it.

8. For Friends and Supporters Asking: How Can I Help?

If you want to be of help, read this book so you will understand the process your buddy is undertaking.

Agoraphobic people recover more easily when they have friends or partners who understand the condition and are supportive. Help beyond that depends on many variables. An important thing to comprehend is that you cannot have expectations about time of recovery. Too many variables. If you are able to help with research as suggested in this book, your time will have been well spent. Do not use any kind of pressure if your partner is working on a Recovery Program. Outside pressure is almost always counterproductive. Communication is important, so plan regular conferences.

As a mental health social worker, I saw many families and relationships torn apart or at least negatively affected by mental illness. I, therefore, advise you to take all steps necessary to preserve your well-being. Doing so could include dramatic changes or even separation from the relationship. This is the hard part, but if you don't take care of yourself, you cannot be of help to anyone else. Agoraphobic people are hypersensitive, and if your participation is not clear and pure and from the heart, you will make matters worse.

Ask what things your friend needs help with, and then be honest with yourself about how much you are willing and able to do. You may be able to help find others inclined to give rides and provide some services. You can also help by coordinating assistance from friends, family members, and neighbors as well as public assistance agencies if necessary. If your friend is going through a homebound phase, you can get extra Saint points by helping to survive it. Help in this case would include bringing in outside necessities, running errands, and being available to assist with baby-step trips outside the safe confines. The dramatic increase in fear that forces an agoraphobe into a corner is demoralizing. Moral support is important during this time. Do what you can.

Here's one bit of agoratrivia that may help you: the circumstances of the initial, panic-inducing event don't really matter because when fear of and avoidance of any one circumstance starts, dominoes fall. Panic attacks in a crowded mall lead a person to avoid not just malls but also any other crowded place. Travel more than a short distance from a safe place can become difficult. Having panic attacks keeps the agoraphobic person on high alert all the time, making it more likely that a panic attack will occur. Yes, while guarding against the feared panic attack, agoraphobes subconsciously create the perfect circumstances for a panic attack. It's complicated.

I hope this explanation helps you more fully understand the person you are close to as well as gives insight to the work involved in changing and redirecting some thought processes in order to get out of the terrible prison of agoraphobia.

And now, let's get started with a plan.

1

GET DOWN TO BUSINESS
A WORKDAY PLAN

To make progress, you need a plan. In order to begin the day-to-day rigors of putting a plan into action, it helps to set some goals. There is so much to gain. To fully appreciate what's at stake here, it might help to take a moment and assess your present situation, and in particular what you have lost.

Living with continual fear and avoidance has taken a toll on your operating system, and it has no doubt left you bankrupt (or nearly so) in many aspects of your life. You may have missed jobs, money, adventures, romances, but most devastating to lose is access to some of the most fulfilling qualities in life: self-confidence and self-respect, courage, strength, insight, balanced mental health, and wisdom.

You have so much to regain:

- **Self-confidence.** When you fail repeatedly to accomplish even seemingly little things, your confidence in your ability to succeed begins to disappear. Rebuild self-confidence by saying affirmations, writing positive statements in your journal, developing your Recovery Program, and teaching yourself skills. And don't forget the adage "Walk like you have money." If you can fool others into thinking you are confident, perhaps you can even convince yourself, and then you will own it.

- **Self-respect/self-esteem.** You are basically a good person, and you like to be truthful, but you have had to make up stories, practice deceit, and sometimes lie outright because of the restrictions your agoraphobia places on you. Seeing disappointed looks from friends, family members, a partner, a boss, and coworkers when you can't participate with them can make you feel low and unworthy. You have probably lost friends because they think you no longer like them. Why else, they wonder, would you avoid being with them so often with lame-sounding excuses? In addition, agoraphobia can use up all your money, and being broke is humiliating. Finally, you feel embarrassed to have such a ridiculous condition in the first place. Regain self-respect through openness exercises, making amends by telling your story, and working hard on your Recovery Program. Practice affirmations and self-love daily. Oh, you beautiful you.

- **Courage.** I won't kid you—it is going to take a tremendous amount of courage for you to take your Very Big Trip. Panic attacks have scared you so many times that you have become fearful of making yourself vulnerable again. It will be easier for you to be courageous if you feel like you can win. What you are working on in this program is developing an *attitude* of winning, a *knowing* feeling. Just saying the word *attitude* gives me one. Try working the word into a mantra. Renew your courage by following through on activities outlined later in this chapter. Include visualization (see chapter 4, "Change Your Own Mind") in your daily routines and you will continue to gain exciting new insights from suggested readings and your own intuitive meanderings.

- **Strength.** You will need spiritual and physical strength to totally overcome excess anxiety. Working hard every day on your Recovery Program will build emotional and spiritual strength and endurance. Meditation can give you a quiet invulnerability. Daily exercises and good nutrition will rebuild your physical core.

- **Insight.** At one time, you may have been good at knowing yourself and knowing what to do to make yourself feel better. Repeated panic attacks and agoraphobia change the rules, however. Now nothing you try seems to help because you quite literally are not yourself. Your daily readings, journaling, and visualizations will help you change some of your thought patterns so you can become once again a person who does not experience panic attacks or anxiety. Everyone but your adrenaline switch operator knows that a panic attack is appropriate only for something as dangerous as the original saber-toothed tiger that started this whole mess in the first place. Your visualization and messaging exercises are drifting into your subconscious so that, along with your research, you will end up with the insight necessary to solve the problem. Insight is not mystical or inborn; it is a skill you can develop through steady study and work—I know because that's how I developed it.

- **Mental health.** You not only are cursed with panic disorder and agoraphobia, which you will cure through the work you are doing, but you likely also suffer from depression. Most therapists would describe the depression that agoraphobic people experience as situational, meaning you are depressed because of your condition. Who wouldn't be? But take heart and remember, panic disorder with agoraphobia is one of the few major mental illnesses that can be completely cured. If you have developed attendant phobias like close places and heights, those will mostly disappear as well when you recover. Once you are over it and are leading a healthy life, you are over it. Mental health is yours to regain.

- **Wisdom.** I believe it is true that people who live through significant trauma, which you are doing, come out of the experience with a wisdom beyond their years. It may seem odd to even think this now, but *you will benefit from this experience.* There, I said it. You probably don't consider yourself wise at this point, because if you were, you would be able to think your way out of agoraphobia. Right? You are gaining wisdom, though, just by dealing every day with your condition. The accumulated knowledge that comes with day-to-day survival and with learning how to cope with and overcome agoraphobia is making you a very wise person; you won't fully realize that until some time after you recover. You are not yet wise enough to overcome your condition, but you will become wise by reading and working on your Recovery Program and developing the basic inner strength that will lead you to make the right decisions and follow the right course. Your wisdom will allow you to be panic-free the rest of your life.

Going to Work—Your New Job

Research shows that we can change our brains. Neural pathways are constructed through regular and vigorous firing of synapses, and new pathways can supplant old ones. Repetitive processes will let the brain know you're going to be doing a lot of work on this highway to freedom; there will be a lot of traffic on a daily basis. To make that possible, you need to establish an "office space" or a "recovery room," a place devoted to this work where you can easily begin your tasks each day.

This space will become a sanctuary for you—a safe place you look forward to being in. Go out of your way to make it feel inviting and comfortable, like a den. It might be just part of a room, but make it feel like a separate space. Outfit it with a table or desk with a table lamp for journal writing and various projects as you choose them. Procure a comfortable chair, preferably one with arms for your exercises, which we'll go over soon. Ideally, you will have a computer and television in this area. If you don't have Internet access, you'll have to rely on the library, a café, or a friend's place for your research. You can do everything else here in your office/recovery room.

I have broken up a typical workday span into hourly blocks as a suggested guide for how you might structure a full day, but you obviously have to do what you can with the life you have. You may only have time to devote a half hour to each area of recovery activity, but do as much as you can in each area each day. This is a job—the-most-important-job-you've-ever-had job. Seriously, brothers and sisters, this is the start of something *very big*.

Hour One—Return of the Endorphins

Agoraphobes are the tightrope walkers in this circus we call life. Yours is a grim task way up there, walking that fine line, fearing you will lose your balance and fall into the abyss if you don't employ all your defenses all of the time. You are dead serious in your day-to-day activities; there is no place for mirth or levity when you are on the high wire trying to keep your pole level. You, my friend, are in a chronic un-endorphined state and must change your ways post-haste. But can a person go from playing such a serious role to becoming a clown? You can and you must, for at least an hour a day.

You will also benefit by learning to *be* funny if you aren't already. It's probably hard to see much humor from your vantage point, but think of your behavior from an alien's point of view. Imagine an alien has been secretly studying human brain activity and behavior, and finally comes to you. "What the . . . ?" the alien might wonder. "What is this weird person up to? And why?" Track your thoughts and movements from the point of view of an alien scientist on a mission, and you might be pretty funny.

The first hour of each new day should be fun, shouldn't it? If you were healthy, you'd be excited most days on waking up because of projects you have going as well as the banquet of opportunities and possibilities that is set before you. Instead, you often wake up with a sense of dread that can easily lead to panic. You wake up not wanting another day, wishing this new day hadn't arrived because you'll have no more control over it than the days before. You get up every morning feeling like you will be ruled by the strong-arm tactics of anxiety all day long.

Luckily, you now have the beginning of a plan that structures the day and will soon put these horrible experiences behind you. You deserve and need a breakfast of laughs and merriment, and YouTube is your kitchen. Comedy is endorphin therapy.[6] Explore old and new comics in their stand-up routines. Check out funny and cute babies and kittens and puppies, watch movies or old TV shows you know will be funny. There are endless hours of endorphin-producing materials online and in the video section of the library, so have a ball. For this first hour of each day, before breakfast, you are required to laugh out loud if it kills you.

There is so much brain science on the health benefits of laughter and merriment, one wonders why we aren't as a society devoting more time to making life hilarious: such as having fun at work. What would be wrong with that? If you'd like to learn more about mental health and positive psychology, go to the Association for Applied and Therapeutic Humor website (*www.aath.org*) where there is a list of nearly one hundred books and articles on the subject.

Hour Two—Pass It Along

This second hour of your day is about finding the ways and means to pass on some of the endorphin-producing joy you've discovered. Start by compiling a list of people who might benefit from a regular cheery call or visit. Your local senior citizen center or nursing home probably employs social workers who can show you how to help connect with a few "shut-ins" who would love someone to chat with for a few minutes every once in a while. A church may also help you contact some people. Get a list of inspirational quotes, jokes, stories, and other such day brighteners that you can share with an elderly or handicapped person. Doing these phone calls will help you get out of your own head and feel like you are contributing to someone's well-being, which you will be. If you're not able to do this kind of work right away, prepare for it now by organizing and gathering what you'll need, and then add it to your routine as soon as possible. You can start by making phone calls until you feel ready to travel and volunteer or do other kinds of outreach. This will benefit you as much as it will others.

Once your Recovery Program is well underway and you get some good ideas for sharing joy in this way, you can start offering helpful hints to folks on agoraphobia online forums. We all need helpful suggestions, so if you come up with something, share it. You could make someone's day. Start sharing yourself instead of hiding yourself.

Hour Three—AgoraGraduate School

You started your day with recess and outreach, so let's hope you are in a good to great mood to begin your classroom studies. This hour of your day will be devoted to a school of your own making—questions, research, reading, listening, and more questions. Spend this time each day exploring aspects of agoraphobia and panic disorder that are new to you. Your research could range from reading a study or discussions online to poring over obscure articles in medical journals. There are many free online university classes. You'll probably find free lectures in the realm of brain science at most of the big universities that have medical schools (Harvard, Stanford, etc.).

Also spend part of this class period reading entries in at least one agoraphobia support forum. Our *www.unagoraphobic.com* website and newsletter will have a forum for you and give you a place to ask questions as well as offer support. The sites *www.MDjunction.com*, *www.supportgroups.com*, and *patient.co.uk* have divisions for agoraphobics. Go to book sites and see what has been published, taking the time to browse through whatever pages are available online before you buy. You might be inspired to take a trip to the bookstore or library for more material. One of my favorite books on the subject of panic disorder and agoraphobia, and a good place to start, is *Life Unlocked* by Dr. Srinivasan Pillay.

As soon as you learn about the support sites, create projects to do during this time. You can create a rough schedule or even a more detailed curriculum to plan the days and weeks ahead. I recommend, for example, you spend one or two sessions studying each of the therapies recommended for agoraphobia in chapter 7, "Call in the Pros: Therapeutic and Legal Help." In fact, you can extend your online studies during this period to any of the topics brought up in this book, from visualization to nutrition and from spirituality to relationships.

As you explore new resources or topic threads online, jot down a few notes about each so you will know how and where to return. Keep study-like notes from your readings in your journal to make this time period feel as much like studying as you can. Even issue a quiz by challenging yourself to summarize an article or topic by recalling its four main ideas. Your job in AgoraGraduate School is to become expert enough in what is known about agoraphobia and panic disorder to understand what you need to change in your thinking processes. The more you know, the more likely you are to make the connection that frees you. This specific knowledge may also prove helpful in explaining yourself to others as the need arises.

As you gain knowledge of the whys and hows of agoraphobia, you can begin to study the wheres, namely the brain. Type *brain science* into your search engine and give yourself time to follow your whims. I am not listing any specific sites because there is so much available; I don't want to place limits on you. Learning how the brain functions helps you visualize your present subconscious behaviors and plan how to make necessary changes in thinking behaviors. After your basic course in neuron pathways, type in *amygdala and anxiety.* This will lead you to mysterious and wonderful websites that range from pure science to the occult.

You remember Indiana Jones?[7] The great professor-explorer character in several adventure movies who stalked dark, scary, mysterious places with his bullwhip? Like him, we must prowl through our jungle of a brain to learn the secret passageway to the decision-making center, the amygdala. If we could just get in there, maybe we could crack the code that reveals how the amygdala decides, with occasional help from the hippocampus,[8] to make one incident alarm worthy and a similar one not. (Now all you need is an ancient map with a big X and a good bullwhip.)

The most important part of this process is to put clear notes in your journal from all your studies. Over time, learn enough about basic brain science so that you could pass a college course. I think you'll find the knowledge adds to the speed with which you'll recover.

Hour Four—Get Physical

Agoraphobics have trouble with breathing so we resist doing exercises that make breathing even more difficult. Add to that being homebound—you may have walked no farther than the mailbox in a long while—and you probably yearn for some kind of exercise that won't take your precious breath away. I recommend starting slowly and getting fit without struggling. Once you begin, the benefits of physical fitness are immediate and ongoing.

All the following are relaxation and strengthening activities that you can mostly do while seated.

Tense and Release

This head-to-toe muscle-relaxation procedure is expanded in chapter 12. Starting with your feet and working up the body, tighten and release your muscles—first feet, then calves, thighs, etc.—breathing in as you tighten and breathing out as you release. Practice this routine on waking up and when you go to bed. I also do a muscle-relaxation routine before starting meditation. For anxious types, learning to meditate can be almost like learning a foreign language, and we need all the help we can get.

Isometrics

Chair exercises can give you a strong core by pitting one group of muscles against another. These are ideal exercises to begin with. Search *isometrics* online to find a routine that will work for you, and here are a few to get you started:

- You can strengthen your abs and thighs by raising one leg at a time until it is parallel to the floor. Do 5 reps with each leg. Breathe in to the count of five as you tighten and out to the count of five as you release throughout the session.

- Make a left-hand fist and bring it in toward you, then cross your right arm over the left wrist and oppose its progress toward you, then swap. This way you can do curls with both arms that will give you solid bicep and triceps muscles.

- Place your palms together in front of you and begin to push one against the other. Count to five, and then curl and grip your fingers so your hands can pull away from each other.

- Grip the sides of your chair seat and push yourself up off it. Do 5 reps.

These last two increase shoulder strength. In all of these routines, breathe slowly and deeply—in as you tighten, out as you release.

Another way to get solid abs involves sitting in a chair and tightening, then releasing muscles. Tighten your abdominal muscles as rigidly as you possibly can, hold for five seconds, breathing all the while as you turn slightly to your left and then slightly to your right. Turn until you feel the tight muscles stretch, and then slowly unflex. Do 30 or more of these a day and you will have solid stomach muscles.

You can also employ yoga and other stretching exercises during this recess, but use caution. Unused muscles need to develop slowly. I used to see a chiropractor whose main income was from yoga injuries.

Take the Stairs

If you have stairs, you can do some aerobic exercise by walking up and down those. You can also exercise even if you only have one step that is safe to step up and down on repeatedly, starting with thirty seconds and working your way up to longer intervals of stepping. That repetition will help your body feel energized without robbing your precious oxygen supply. If you start slowly, you can get fit without struggling, and finally one day you will realize your breathing is free and easy for a change. At that point, you can ride your bike or do power walking or jogging.

Time for Lunch

A traditional soup, salad, and sandwich is always a good choice. Find much more on health and nutrition in chapter 6, "Eat (While) Nuts—and Also Berries."

Hour Five—New Skills: Oh Yes, You Can!

This one is *mandatory:* learn a new skill. In this hour, you will embark on an exciting part of your Recovery Program that will give you a new dimension, make you a more interesting person, and grant you full use of your powers of creativity.[9] Whatever you decide to do, this activity will give you increased use of the right hemisphere of your brain, the creating side, and become part of your meditative healing process. By learning a new skill, you will learn how to think of yourself as *creative,* thereby allowing the creative part of you to become a *force.* Having the power of creativity at your fingertips will greatly assist your healing process. I remember hoping that working in artistic areas would help heal me, and now I know I was right. I think it was intuition telling me that.

Think carefully about the skill you are going to learn, as it may very well be something you do with interest for the rest of your life. This could be something novel to you, something you may never have even thought of doing, or it could be something you've dreamed of doing for years. In my case, learning to draw was something I'd long wanted to achieve. Select a skill you can do within or near the confines of your office/recovery room. This new skill should be something that doesn't make a huge mess, it should be something you can start and stop in short order, and it should be something you can mostly teach yourself. Your new skill should be something that requires your total concentration all the time you are doing it. Most importantly, it should be something whose complexity can increase as your skills improve, something you can never tire of because you can make it more challenging through your own creativity and desire for mastery. Make it your goal to become very good at what you are learning. Following are some suggestions for your new skill hour:

Drawing, Painting, and Small Sculpture

Small arts activities can easily fit in your space. Find a way to spend an hour in a bookstore so you can prowl through the arts and crafts and how-to section for ideas. Buy a book that will give you most of what you need in order to begin your new identity. There is also free online instruction in all the traditional arts. Drawing and painting will get you into your right brain, especially if you draw or paint from models or photographs or from a still life. Any of the Drawing on the Right Side of the Brain series of books by Betty Edwards will give you the skills you need.[10] There are similar painting books. All are available in your bookstores or library. Small wax sculptures or stone or wood carvings could also work as a meditative tool— especially if the task totally takes your thoughts away.

I highly recommend drawing as a healing tool because it worked so well for me. I started drawing during a particularly difficult, anxious time when I desperately needed some diversions. It was during the second night of drawing faces of musicians from record album covers with an old pencil on copy paper that I realized I was engaged in a form of meditation. Two hours passed unnoticed, and I discovered with delight that I could become a calm person again just by doing specific drawing exercises. Learning to draw takes learning to *see* in a new way. You begin to look at everything with curiosity and objectivity as you get even a little proficient in drawing. After you have been drawing for a while, you will connect with the world around you in a new, objective way that helps you replace your fears with calm analysis of a particular situation.

Instead of constantly scanning everything around me, I could now pause and *notice* specific things. The new pencil-wielding me was thinking, for example, *The person in that doorway must be a dancer with that graceful stance.* This calm, appraising attitude I had suddenly learned was a welcome replacement for my usual subconscious routine of rapidly evaluating the things around me for their danger potential.

Playing a Musical Instrument

If you would like to become musical and have no experience with an instrument, try learning to play the penny whistle, a harmonica, or the recorder. I suggest these because they are inexpensive, easy enough to learn, and can play a full range of music. Learning one of these instruments will help you with better cognitive functioning as well as breathing. Most other instruments are too complicated to learn or too big, loud, or expensive for these purposes. (Even these little instruments can be loud, so you have to allow for that.) If you can afford one, guitars make good lifetime companions. Who better than you to write the song "I Got Them Cabin Fever Blues"? I've always thought playing the marimba would be a soothing thing to do. Perhaps a small hand drum would be your magic potion. You could also learn to sing while you play. Once you learn how to play and read music for one instrument, you can more easily learn other instruments.

Learning to read music is a good right-brain activity, but it is said that music uses all the brain. A *National Geographic* article in the January 2014 issue on music and the brain cited studies indicating that learning to play music is beneficial to the brain no matter when you start and that a Harvard University neurologist discovered that brains of adult professional musicians had significantly more gray matter and white matter than nonmusicians' brains and were more plastic (the ability for the brain to make changes in how it works). The same article told of a University of Florida music professor who tested elderly piano students before and after a year or so of lessons and found the students had improved cognitive abilities as well as speed of processing information.

Fiber Arts

The fiber arts include a number of skills you can teach yourself. Check your bookstores for how-to fiber books, or learn in a class or online. Taking a class would be helpful to you because of the social and learning opportunity. Knitting is an obvious activity you could learn and practice wherever you go. People I know who knit say they find the activity calming and meditative. If your new skill becomes too easy, its purpose can be defeated, so something like knitting, which can certainly grow increasingly complex, is great. Embroidery, lace making, and other fancy stitch work as well as decorative beading and felting are good skills to know, and you might even make money with them once you can travel to craft fairs. If you want to learn to sew, a machine can easily fit into your space.

If you can acquire a table loom, you could become a weaver of intricate pieces. Weaving of small baskets is a tremendously absorbing and calming activity. Quilting is a traditional craft that progresses from very simple designs to complex, intricate patterns that can be hand- or machine-sewn.

Jewelry Making

Making jewelry through true fabrication, meaning making at least some of the parts on your own, requires intense concentration. I'm referring to things like silversmithing, clay and glass beadmaking, scrimshaw, and the like. As a reminder, skills you have to work hard to learn are skills that will heal you. For these purposes, just stringing beads will not require the kind of therapeutic focus I want you to realize.

Making small sculptures or jewelry from any of the colored oven-baked clays can require intense focus, depending on complexity, and can result in beautiful products. You can create mind-blowing intricate patterns by layering and slicing various colors. You can more easily express whimsy with soft oven clay than any other medium. Sculpey brand oven-bake clay, for example, offers forty-four colors. Designing and laying out patterns for jewelry pieces can take your mind away from everything else.

No matter what you want to learn, there are how-to books in your local bookstore or library. You'll also find free teachers on YouTube and other sites, covering virtually every aspect of jewelry making. If jewelry isn't exciting for you, an activity that shares some of the skill and challenge is tying flies (for fly-fishing), which is a hobby that can also become profitable.

Writing

This is another skill you could learn and have fun doing the rest of your life. Writing takes many forms—from poetry to epic novels to journalism to essays. Fiction writing comes naturally to the agoraphobe because our imaginations are always running wild. You have probably thought of a travel adventure or a detective novel starring you, or a romance that totally worked out or . . . there is no limit to what you could write because you're making it all up.

One of the immediate benefits of starting to write is that when you are developing a story idea, you will have plenty to think about at bedtime to replace your stinkin' thinkin'. Writing seriously may become something you want to pursue after you recover, but for now think of writing as therapy; your chance to vent a little or explain yourself in a new light. Here is your opportunity to know what it is like to stare at a blank screen or piece of paper and begin a great adventure, to create a world that didn't exist until you sat down and made it appear. There is something very engaging about starting a story, so if that appeals to you, you can spend this hour in fantasy land. I may someday find you signing your books at a bookstore. Make an outline for your book and a list of characters to get you started. Your life is good material.

If writing at length doesn't appeal to you, try short stories or essays. Write stories about some of the odd people you've met, including relatives. Perhaps you would rather be a poet, your pen poised over your notebook beside a cup of tea in the corner of a café.

Writing poetry to a particular rhyme or meter pattern is skill and art in equal measure and demands total focus. Completing a poem gives a rewarding and satisfying feeling. There's no need to be squeamish when it comes to poetry—there are poems, and poets, of all kinds.

I recommend writing haiku poetry, not only as an activity for this hour but also as a device to use in a stressful time, when panic threatens. Find a haiku book so you can read enough of these particular poems to know what you can do with the form. The process of creating haiku is, essentially, a meditative experience (with counting syllables) that you can start doing whenever you are feeling anxious. In fact, writing haiku is a perfect tool for an agoraphobe because forming one requires you to be studying your immediate environment very closely, linking in, which brings you out of the anxiety swirling in your own head.

In choosing a subject for a haiku, you are looking for something that is striking—something in your world that is beautiful or unusual or magical or just odd in some way. Something you see or feel *grabs* you, and you want to say something about it. A haiku poem is usually an expression of something in the natural world, but it can also be born out of an experience in your nature. The poem is expressed through a specific formula of seventeen total syllables: the first line is five syllables, the second line is seven syllables, and third line is five syllables. Don't cheat on the formula. I'm very strict about that. The process of writing haiku will take your mind off everything else.

I've written a lot of haiku; this is one of my favorites:

Weaver plucks a hair

Whose golden strand joins the weft

For her lover's scarf

If I had known during times of extreme anxiety what I know now, I would have been walking around half that time with my lips moving and fingers flying, counting syllables, as I kept anxiety at bay. Now I understand that the periods of time when I made *creative* thinking all of my thinking (as while writing or drawing), I was moving my brain processes further and further away from my old system of frantic hypervigilance. Being creative was increasing my self-confidence.

Speaking a Foreign Language

Learning a new language is another way to make good use of this hour. Speaking a foreign tongue requires the focus and attention to detail similar to many physical skills you might learn, and it does not require tools. You can purchase computer programs for language learning at your bookstore or get them from the library. Free online foreign language instruction is also available.

Whatever this new skill is, remember that you will be doing it a lot, so if your interest wanes, quickly try something new. Have a few choices, but don't make that an excuse to never concentrate on one thing.

Hour Six—Remodel Time (This Old Brain)

This is the hour of each day during which you will be doing remodeling work on your brain so that you won't have to search through graveyards to find an entirely new one. You will use this time for positive thinking exercises and visualizations, sending messages over and over in order to persuade the stubborn holder of false notions (the subconscious) to learn the truth that shall free the prisoner (you).

Begin by reflecting on and writing about the Thought Police actions today (see chapter 4 for a description of these guys). Write down the negative thoughts you encountered and the positive thoughts you parried with. Create a couple of new mantras to use tomorrow that are specific to something you are working on. For example, "I don't have to worry about crossing the bridge today because I'll be thinking about bluebirds going over a rainbow while I whistle that song on my drive." You just invented the whistling mantra. Then write a paragraph about one positive thing that happened today.

When you have finished your Positive Thinking work, put down your pen and begin your visualization session. See chapter 4, "Change Your Own Mind: Positive Thinking and Visualization," where I have suggested in the visualization section some exercises and techniques to help you send new kinds of messages, which will eventually change some of the patterns of thinking that are creating your problem.

Relax, close your eyes, and create your new brain.

Hour Seven—Journaling and Recovery Plan Think Tank

This is the time of day to measure your progress (or regress, let's be honest) by putting the day into words and numbers, and to plan for tomorrow. Review writings and memories from each of your work sessions as well as from everything else that happened today, and make a statement to yourself about how you are feeling about what you are doing in your recovery. Here is an example of what could be a typical entry: "I learned some very helpful stuff I didn't know about my one trigger on way to work and started work to defuse it. Still have terrible period of anxiety just before noon. Need to work on breathing and on-site muscle relaxation. Don't know for sure if program's working—still lots of anxiety. Doing this creates anxiety sometimes. Need to work harder on diversions in skill learning." Brief phrases that summarize various aspects of your recovery are easy to write and easy to compare day to day.

When you finish your summary, write a few notes about what you will work on tomorrow. For example, "Return to *brainsciencepodcast.com* to finish neuron study; start day with adding to list of avoidances to work on; print out music for song to learn . . ." and on from there. Planning for tomorrow's activities will help you stay focused and give you positive things to think about as you go to sleep tonight. I always feel that my subconscious will get some of my work done if I give it specific assignments, and science seems to agree.

The value of clear and comprehensive language in your journal entries will soon become apparent. That doesn't mean you have to be fussy with grammar. As you begin to develop your Recovery Program, you will want to look back at earlier entries to see how and what you were doing at a particular time. If you wrote clearly enough about your feelings and condition, you will benefit from the information.

For example, say you were having a hard time last week and on Wednesday you wrote, "Feeling extra anxious about 10 every morning for several days with extra trouble breathing." The next day, you started a routine of taking a break from work a little before ten to do some breathing and relaxation exercises and then some positive mantras or chants for a while before returning to work. After two weeks of doing the new action, you would like to know if your new routine is working by comparing you now to you two weeks ago. If you used numbers to describe anxiety levels, as you'll learn about in the following "Order" section, and the right words to describe feelings and circumstances, you have useful data that will help you recover. If your techniques are working for you, enhance and embellish them so you will have a broad range of ways to recover.

That's sort of the science part of your writing project. The other part should focus on the voice of your heart. What do I mean by this? I mean passion. What you are experiencing as an agoraphobe is fraught with passion, if you think of passion as something to do with experiencing and maybe expressing the strongest of feelings. Suffering and agony are the first emotions mentioned in my Webster's definition of *passion*, but there are of course equally positive associations with passion.

You are experiencing feelings of an intensity that not one in a thousand people experiences. The fullness of your passion (now taking the form of anxiety, panicky feelings, extreme discontent, and even desperation) will continue to be part of your life in a positive way (inspiration, connection, fervor, excitement) long after your recovery, probably forever. You will forever be a passionate person because of the way you are and the enormity of what you're going through.

You are having a life-altering experience that feels so extreme, probably only people who have had severe life-altering experiences themselves could comprehend it. Your depth of passionate feeling will be as significant a part of you as any extraordinary dramatic occurrence would. Write about your life with the same bewilderment and fear and anger and passion that you felt and feel. Go about this slowly and safely, however. You can even record these feelings in the third person if you like; for example, "The victim could feel rivulets of sweat running down her armpits as she waited for the train to pass." This technique allows you to act as an observer but still reveal the actual feelings.

Your New Job Description

So what is it that you're doing with this daily plan? And why is writing it all down so essential? Your job is to completely and totally reverse everything about fear that controls you now; in other words, completely and totally reverse the way you *think* about fear. Think you can do it? It means totally letting down your guard and allowing the thing you dread the most to come sit beside you on the couch. Yesterday you perceived this "thing" as the most gruesomely dangerous and fear-provoking whatever-it-is in the whole universe. You were deathly afraid of it, just yesterday, and tried to avoid it like it was the plague, and today you're expected to just sit down and be best pals with it?

Admittedly, doing so won't be easy because you are so heavily conditioned to fear a mad variety of circumstances and conditions, any of which could trigger a panic attack even though they present no actual danger to you. What you actually fear is having fearful feelings and emotions. You're conditioned to fear fear, which is everywhere when mostly all you feel is fearful.

This would be comical if it weren't so serious. (You do get to laugh later.)

We make up our minds, and then we change our minds thousands of times. Hundreds of times each day, we make a decision, judgment, or observation that we have to adjust later on as we gather more data and gain more knowledge. We change our minds. It's easy. We have to, otherwise . . . well, we have to. The thing is, I *know* I can change my mind. Therefore, I know you can change your mind.

This is where your creativity can kick in: I'll start it with a question. I'm a fifth-grade teacher, and I ask, "Will you explain to my students in class tomorrow exactly what it is you have and what they can do to avoid getting it?" This can be one of your early journal entries and an answer you can revisit and revise as you build your Recovery Program. Writing this down—simply explaining in terms a child can understand what it is that you have—should be eye-opening. Save what you write and maybe we can put together a compilation of *Stories to Fifth Graders from Agoraphobes* someday. Stay tuned at *www.unagoraphobic.com*.

I'm writing this to point out to you that the more you write about your daily passions (negative and positive), the more you will understand yourself. The more you understand yourself and your own story, the richer your life will be. I wouldn't take it lightly, this unusual opportunity you have for personal and spiritual growth that arises because of all this madness. I wish I had written more during my sputtering, wandering recovery so I could have a fuller, *written* understanding of what I'm made of.

You're going through this, so you might as well learn everything you can from it and use the experience for something worthwhile. In fact, you can make as much use of this whole saga as you choose to. I chose to write a book and will continue to do more writing. Many of you will end up doing good work of some kind. Your ability to engage in acts of compassion might not have come so easily to you if you had been on a less drama-filled path.

2

DEVELOP A
WRITING HABIT

Remember, you will recover from agoraphobia by
restoring your self-confidence and courage through
research and daily work to reprogram your subconscious so that you no longer fear having a panic attack.
The more you learn about your affliction, the greater
the likelihood you will discover the way to set yourself free. In your journal, you are quite literally writing
the manual of your own recovery; your journal reflects
what you learn and what you feel and will be your
resource material and your guidebook. Writing gives
permanent voice to your thoughts, ideas, and discoveries. What's more, the act of writing helps create new
neural pathways, changing the makeup of your brain.[11]

I think you will enjoy journaling, but even if you
do not enjoy writing at all, my hope is that you will
use the safety and anonymity of journal writing as a
release of feelings as well as to improve your writing skills and make yourself more comfortable with

this form of communication. Get several notebooks; you'll probably fill them quickly.

Think of writing as a tool to explain your feelings to yourself. Think of writing regularly in your journal as being your own shrink. If you already enjoy writing, keeping this journal will be a way for you to explore new ways of expressing your ideas as well as to discover your writing style. Don't shortchange the process by allowing yourself to become too breezy. Fully express yourself in creative ways. No matter where you are with writing, you will become more confident as you improve, which you will day by day.[12]

Begin your journal with a two-part statement about you. In Part A, write conversationally about how you think it happened that you ended up being agoraphobic. This could be the narrative for your story to a fifth grader. Probe into this. After all, you're not crazy, as in delusional, but the way you think has led you to become at least partially disabled. As your own shrink, ask yourself some significant questions. *What is the history of my excessive or inappropriate anxiety? Do I have a theory of how it started? Was there high anxiety in the home or similar environment?* Describe it. Be as specific and objective as you can while writing this. Describe your anxiety as though you were talking with a psychiatrist who mostly wants to hear about feelings. Don't make this the story of your life but rather the story of why you feel so fearful that you are ruining your life.

Part B of the first-day essay is to dream and plan your life after you recover. This will be a thoughtful extension of the bedtime story from the introduction—remember the one where the prince/princess (you) was locked away in a tower? Now it's time to write the "happily ever after." Talk about the changes you want to make when you are free to roam about. Do you want to move? Change jobs? Change almost everything? Or do you simply want to "change" by managing to return to what you were happily doing before you were so rudely interrupted? Write about the new world that awaits you and what you plan to do with your new life. Write some goals, but don't make anything time specific. Think of this opening two-part statement you're writing as the "before" in "before and after."

Here are some suggestions on how to make your journal work for you. I have also included a sample day's journal entry afterward.

Organization

Make your first notation as soon after arising as you can. Review yesterday's entry and then record the time you went to sleep, hours slept, and quality of sleep using a 0 to 10 scale (10 being the best). Then rate your current anxiety level with the same scale and get on with your day. Here is an example of how to start a day's entry. Draw a line across the top of the page, and above the line, write the date and the four key numbers: "Bedtime 12:30, Hours sleep 6 1/3, Quality sleep 2 (rotten, restless), Anxiety level 4." Be sure to give your anxiety level a closing number before you go to bed. Write "Endorphin Hour" below the line, and write about your experiences and feelings while you're laughing your cares away in the first hour of the day. Do the same for each of the work periods throughout the day. This is like college. Study hard and take good notes, because you're going to have to answer some difficult questions.

You may want to wait until later in the day to write about some of the hands-on activities, but if anything particularly stirs you, I recommend noting it at the time it is stirring you. Most agoraphobic people I have encountered tend to the orderly side, so far be it from me to show you how to organize your journal beyond what I've just said. The only advice I'd give is to make sure your process is extremely user-friendly so that later on, when your journaling motivation might not be so high, you will still be able to enter data of some usefulness.

Writing Voice

Writing gives voice to your thoughts; therefore, your writing should sound like you. Writing conversationally doesn't come easily to everyone, but once you learn to write as you speak, your communication skills will improve immensely. It's one of those things that you finally figure out how to do, like whistle through your fingers, and then you can always do it. Reading your writing aloud can help make it sound more natural. Also listen carefully to the way others speak. The very best advice I can give a writer, however, is to let passion rule. This journal is all about you, so if you are happy or sad or scared or enlightened, your journal will reflect it if you write it as you feel it.

If journaling leads you to want to continue writing, one book I always recommend to would-be writers is *The Elements of Style* with E. B. White as one of the editors (Strunk and White).[13] It's a small book but tells you everything you need to know about the rules of writing in a charming and humorous way. (Not that you need to follow "rules" in your journal.)

Details, Details

Use detail and descriptions throughout your writing to give visual dimension to all your experiences and to make them easier to recall. Use all your senses when you are recalling and recording. For example, what was the weather like when you tried to travel today? Did the heat or chill contribute to your tension? What did the world smell like? What and who did you see on your way? Tie everything together with details so your entry feels like a real live day with real live events and happenings that made it unlike any other day.

How to Rite Good

This is *your* journal, so it doesn't have to be grammatically correct, of course. There won't be grading. I recommend, though, that you use this opportunity to work on your writing skills. Write strong, declarative sentences in an active voice that reflect your feelings and give vent to your emotions; this is one way you will discover things about yourself that will help in your recovery. I often don't fully comprehend my feelings on a particular subject until I start writing about it. Not surprisingly, as you write, you improve your writing ability, making your writing more interesting to read and thus easier to pore over weeks down the road for help in tracking your levels. Also, you are going to be looking back at today's writing at some point in the future, so you will want to be clear about what you have said. Good writing is like a mountain stream—clear and free flowing.

Your words can be emotionally powerful for you. Think of choice words spoken or written by others that you remember because they stirred you. You can cause a strong emotional response in yourself with your own words, and you can use your own words to transform your thinking processes. This is my way of saying, "Tell it like you mean it." Do not censor yourself.

For Straight Men Only (Confidential)

That's right. What I'll be saying in this section is of interest to heterosexual males only, so if you aren't one, you can go on to something else and stop reading now because there is nothing here for you. Plus, this is a *secret* I'm revealing to straight males.

Pssssst. Hetero men! I can reveal to you the answer to one of the great mysteries of the Universe: what women want. One of women's most valid life complaints is that men can't, or won't, talk to them about *feelings*. How true, how true. At no extra charge, *Un-agoraphobic* will give each male reader an edge with women, if you want one. The work you are doing here will make it impossible for you *not* to talk about your feelings. What do women want? They want you to *talk* with them—about feelings, about day-to-day activities, about gossip, about anything and everything, to talk about *Life*. Journaling here will give you that skill. Have you ever noticed that a lot of straight women adore gay men? Can you guess why? It's the talking, stupid. Now, as a result of this recovery program, women have *you* to talk with. Again, no extra charge.

Sample Day in Journal

April 14

Bed: 2 a.m.   Hrs. slp: 7   Qlty slp: 6   Anx lvl: 5

Endorphin hour: Watched equal amounts of kitty pranks and little kids—very adorable. Saw great old episode of "Pushing Daisies"—hysterical. Finished with "Hollywood Squares" bloopers—laughed aloud, very good laugh. Hard to allow myself this much goofing off time, but think it helps. Might be half a point happier. More laughing babies tomorrow—the ultimate antidote to despair.

Outreach: Had a great talk with Elmer from Hill Park Retirement. Asked him if he'd ever had anxiety, and he told me some real war stories that made my anxiety feel minor. Totally different kind of anxiety, but good to hear another perspective. Read some old entries in online forum to learn what people have been talking about over time. Not much seems to change there.

Research: Good to learn about role of hippocampus vs. amygdala. Helps to visualize messages. Wonder if agoraphobes more prone for some reason to mixed messages from amygdala. Something we're born with? Look that up. Look up *tryptophan* tomorrow. Causes sleepiness? Nothing I've been researching has created anxiety so far. This is good diversion—but need to find more articles, or better yet a book, on confidence building.

Workout: Found some videos on exercises for reducing back pain—got down on floor to do those. Need some kind of pad—see if Owen has one. Did the bicep curls and doing more abs exercises—part of back program. Ran up stairs twice in row and after rest twice again. Did couple minutes deep breathing—still kind of tight for full deep breath. Didn't meditate, but closed eyes during breathing. Felt pulse and tried to slow it by meditation thoughts.

Skills: Still can't decide between penny whistle and harmonica. Easier to pick out tunes on whistle, but prefer harmonica sound. Maybe learn harmonica after learning music on whistle. Reading music is harder than thought it would be. Good to play music, good to know you can start learning any time. Don't forget grandpa's guitar in sister's basement. Have to learn to relax more while playing—not let bloopers bother me—just keep playing. Tomorrow learn music reading. Learn one short tune.

Remodel: I did kind of a treasure hunt visualization last night—kept me awake awhile, but it was very relaxing doing the walk through the woods imagery. Put up Post-It notes today saying, "Halt!" to remind me of Thought Police. Been forgetting last couple of days to think about thoughts. This morning realized I'd been thinking about some way to cancel going to family picnic Saturday instead of thinking of some way to get there, which I'm now thinking about positively when I remember. This remembering-thought stuff is hard, but it's helping me stay positive. I can feel that for sure. Got this great idea for dialogue w/ switchmeister. I come to this great hall where I've put her in a small side room like Wiz of Oz. I've been sneaking up on her and saying, "Boo!" And then hiding. Working my way up to saying boo and daring her to push button. Wooo. Scary. Maybe I should be more adult. Anyway . . .

Working on the trip to work. My visualization is I'm connected on a 30-foot pole to the car ahead of me on the bridge, so I can just imagine totally relaxing on the ride over because

I don't have to brake or accelerate or steer. Motivation is: sick of going to work an hour early to avoid traffic. I'm feeling good about visualization stuff because it appeals to my kind of spiritual self—sort of a faith that doing this really changes stuff in my brain.

Recovery Program: I woke up with a jolt this morning, before the alarm and frantic thoughts kept me from going back to sleep. How can I learn to love that? Tried to stay positive and think about little problem-solving things for today—very constructive thoughts. Getting okay with brief stretching and breathing session before getting out of bed. Didn't really even think about coffee this morning—quick glass of ice water helps quell urge (just making that up).

Taken to reading old *New Yorker*s from the library donation table during breakfast—more calming than the newspaper or the screen. Had great laughs on YouTube today—even started snorting. Reminder to self: Get some vids from library so I can watch TV for break from computer.

Don't feel like I've developed my own "plan" yet, but it feels good to be working on getting over this. Working on some of this stuff is a diversion but can also create some anxiety, which makes me resist working on certain issues. Guess that means I should work harder or stay with the ideas that scare me and start anxiety. But I'm a chicken, so what do I do? I'll find out tomorrow when I start again. The best thing is I look forward to starting routine each day. Anxiety level 4.5.

3

FIND INNER QUIET
A FEW MINDFULNESS TOOLS THAT GO A LONG WAY

Spirituality can present unique problems for people with panic disorder. The subject came up from time to time at the various peer support groups I was involved in over the years, but I never heard anyone in those groups claim they were cured of agoraphobia through religion. A belief system may have helped some, but the whole issue of religious spirituality is touchy in a diverse group setting, so religion per se did not come up often. While many in the groups said they felt a need for a spiritual identity of some sort, some agoraphobic people don't want to even *think* about spiritual matters—they need this life to be concrete, solid, *real,* in the face of their paralyzing fear.

The mysteries in my personal world, for example, were often so overwhelming and troubling that larger cosmic questions struck terror in my heart. When I was in my teens, I could not think about the

Universe, period. I never looked up at the night sky (talk about wide open spaces) and, after a long time of praying fruitlessly for relief from panic attacks, I pretty much became an atheist. I know there are some people whose belief in a deity provides comfort and relief from anxiety, but traditional religion does not work for everyone. Instead, I created a number of little fictions and fantasies to help me survive youthful periods of intense anxiety and help me create a safe niche in this world without the scary mystery of God.

The Buddha Path

When I became intellectually capable of searching for answers to my anxiety problems, I discovered Buddhism. I began to feel comfort as soon as I started reading the story of young, sheltered Siddhartha Gautama, so deeply affected by the misery and suffering he saw around him in India about 2,500 years ago that he left his wealthy family behind and devoted the rest of his life to learning and teaching in order to help people lead better lives. There was no creation story and no sense of a deity to make me feel I was on unsure footing.[14] What I read about Buddhism seemed to me very human, very real, and very possible.

The inspiration of his example gave me comfort: humans can heal themselves through meditation leading to enlightenment, leading to selflessness and generosity. More importantly, though, it gave me *hope*. I finally realized I could have some influence on my own bewildering fearfulness and needn't depend on the mystery of any kind of divine intervention. Hope was something I had lost so gradually over the years that I didn't know how low I was until this particular realization. After that, I knew I had the power to essentially change my way of thinking because of the positive charge I'd suddenly developed.

Siddhartha taught his wisdom to others as he traveled. His ways to end suffering were so inspiring and influential that they were passed along in the oral tradition through the country.[15] Buddhism became a way for people to feel hopeful, to put meaning in their lives, and to end their misery through meditation. Going on the Buddha path showed people a way to achieve a peaceful mind and enjoy harmony with the Universe. Give somebody a sound plan and hope, and they can accomplish whatever they want.

Many years passed between my very first comforting readings in Buddhism and my realization that Buddhism is actually a *perfect model* for recovery from panic disorder. First, its stated purpose is to end suffering—who more than us agoraphobes would buy a ticket for that? Even the *thought* that I could end my suffering was helpful, giving me hope and allowing me to feel better about myself. Second, Buddhism focuses on mindfulness—bringing your full concentration to the present problem in the present moment—as a means to make your life better.[16] As it turns out, this is also the absolute definition of your Recovery Program.

It has been demonstrated that the use of mindfulness can change neural pathways in your brain.[17] The way you are going to become free from agoraphobia is by devoting your entire focus to inventing your solution, right here in the present moment.

The Buddhist spiritual leader Tenzin Gyatso, the Fourteenth Dalai Lama, has participated in several conferences involving scientists and scholars in studies of the effects of mindfulness on the brain. Of the brain change studies on neuroplasticity he said, "They have the potential to be of practical importance in our understanding of education, mental health and the significance of ethics in our lives."[18] He makes the connection unmistakable in this writing, remarking, "It is a fundamental Buddhist principle that the human mind has tremendous potential for transformation."

In my opinion, you do not have to *become* a Buddhist to use some of the principles to help you recover from agoraphobia. You don't have to be an official Buddhist to be Buddha-like. I'm not a Buddhist; if anything I'm a humanist, by which I mean one who focuses on the achievements of humans through self-determination as opposed to divine influence.[19] It's worth taking the time to prowl through your favorite bookstore for a nice book on Buddhism, something you'll probably refer to often through the years.

What I'm saying is, you don't have to *be something* in order to feel safe and connected to your world. You don't have to be a member of any group in order to belong to the big club of human beings who belong to the even bigger club of living things. We have to learn to love (or at least accept) one another, because we all live in the same building. My biggest complaint about religion is it separates us so. Buddhism calls itself the "middle way" and is there for anyone to study and use in order to improve their lives. The Buddha wanted his followers to avoid extremes and established the "middle path" as a self-imposed guide for moral conduct, a path one would follow because of the value of leading such a life, not because of dictated teachings involving strict rules, worship, and prayer.

Buddhist teachings have been bundled into a package that includes beliefs and practices like yoga, karma, and reincarnation, which were already being practiced when Siddhartha was born. In some ways, it's a bit of a catch-all, and I recommend you study Buddhism and take from it what will be of most help to you. I found many recovery tools just by reading and pondering the Eight-Fold Path, as related in *The Buddhist Handbook*.[20] I will briefly summarize the three basic structures (wisdom, morality, and discipline) of the Eight-Fold Path below in a way that will help you see how they apply to overcoming panic attacks and agoraphobia:

Prajna

Prajna is the wisdom that purifies the mind, allowing it to attain spiritual insight into the true nature of things. This is what you are doing with your daily studies, especially of brain function and science as they relate to your panic attack problem. When you discover the true nature of your panic button, you will be on your way to controlling it, by viewing reality as it is, not as it appears to be. That's insight, which becomes wisdom.

Sila

Sila is the ethics or morality that prevents a person from performing unwholesome deeds. When you complete your Recovery Program, you will be a changed person and will discover that you must live an upright, open, honest (especially to yourself) life in order to stay healthy. Speaking and acting truthfully and in nonharmful ways will become part of your character, if they are not already. They probably are. I've never met an unkind agoraphobic person. We are nice to people in the Golden Rule way because we never know when we may need their help.

Samadhi

Samadhi is the mental discipline required to develop mastery over one's mind and is achieved through practice of various contemplative and meditative disciplines. Making an effort to improve is part of the Buddha Path work, and developing your Recovery Program means you are improving your abilities and knowledge in a variety of disciplines. You are already doing daily meditative work in your skills-learning hour, but sitting in meditation will help you see things more clearly and improve your ability to do your messaging and visualization work.

There are four aspects to Buddhism that were of tremendous help in my recovery, and I will describe them below. Please note that I'm not claiming to properly represent Buddhism. My interpretations may not always match the writings of others, but I think I understand the essence of the concepts. The practice of Buddhism has become highly decorated with rituals and ceremonies, but since I've never been much of a joiner, I always study aspects of things to see what I can take away that will be helpful to me. In other words, I interpreted Buddhism for my own needs in order to create useful tools for getting over agoraphobia. The following tools led to my escape, and they still work for me.

Meditation

Spending part of each day eliminating all but the present moment will help you soothe your savage beast. Through some form of meditation, you will learn to let all random thoughts pass on by until you are able to concentrate solely on one thought or just on your breathing—hypnotically focusing on the coming and going of air from your lungs. Going from panicky anxiety to quiet meditation can be a difficult journey. I found that if I did my toe-to-head tense-and-release muscle relaxation beforehand, I could more easily reach a meditative state. The exercise not only calmed me down, but it also helped me focus.

Breathing is a problem for people with anxiety and panic attacks. Improving your ability to breathe through meditation will noticeably reduce your tension, which is a big step on the road to recovery. You know that your stomach muscle, the diaphragm, controls your breathing, and you know how calming a deep breath is. (Sometimes it seemed like I went days without one. Needlessly, needless to say.) To breathe in, allow your stomach to protrude, and your lungs will inflate automatically. The problem anxious people have is that all their muscles are tight and nothing flows freely.

When you are tight, you tend to breathe shallowly, never expelling all the carbon dioxide. This actually makes you more anxious. Don't freak out about it; just stick your gut way out and breathing will happen, giving you better things to think about. I recall trying to suck in air like a beached fish during particularly tense times. Anxious people are always *trying* to breathe instead of just breathing. Breathing is controlled by the part of the brain that doesn't need to be told to do things, so get out of its way.

In the beginning, pick your calmest part of day (mine was late afternoons) to give yourself the ideal time to do this exercise of letting go. Once you learn that meditating is safe and you get the hang of it, I recommend scheduling it at your most stressful time, where it might do the most good. Start by getting seated in an upright, comfortable position on a pad or chair, and close your eyes. You don't have to, but if you can comfortably sit on the floor and fold your feet that yogi way, lucky you. Your goal is to eliminate all the noise in your brain and be only in the moment. Focus intently on your breathing, in through the nose and out through the mouth. Home in, for example, on the sensation inside your nostrils and on your tongue as you breathe in to the count of four and breathe out through your slightly parted lips to the count of eight.

Deflect random thoughts by turning them into balloons and watching them float away, as is suggested in many meditation writings. Feel your body loosen and get comfortable as a regular breathing rhythm continues. The main problem Westerners have with meditation is *it doesn't feel like you're doing anything.* Duh. Practice sitting in meditation every day for at least ten minutes at a time and you will improve your ability to get into that calming place. Once you get accustomed to slipping into the safe haven of meditation, you learn to trust that you will always have a safe haven when anxiety threatens.

If you cannot yet sit in meditation, there are many other ways of being meditative, some of which involve activities as presented in your daily work routine. As I said in the first chapter, doing drawing exercises became meditation time for me, and hours passed without notice. Still, there's nothing like sitting and breathing to both simplify and edify your new life. That sounds wonderful, doesn't it? *Your new life.* Do an online search for meditation styles and find something that works for you. Having this skill will be of great help in deflecting panic attacks.

Simplicity (Gateway to Creativity)

The most basic of life's concepts, like simplicity, become profound because they have so much meaning to modern humans. It can take a lot of complex seeking to find simplicity. During my years with panic attacks, I yearned for simple thinking—to be able to just sit and ponder at length about one tree in the park, or nothing at all—but I found it impossible to still my mind to do so.

Why is simplicity so critical for your recovery? Because you are, frankly, a scatterbrain and need to learn to sit in repose and evaluate things and ideas as they come to you. Imagine that. Just you, calmly going about your day in a place of your choosing, taking each thing as it's handed to you, and being able to make a cool, rational decision about each thing—because at that particular moment, that's all you have to do. Your life is simple. *You don't have to clutter up your brain by anticipating everything.*

I don't want to get too deep about the subject of simplicity, but it seems like our world got so complex so fast (particularly in the last hundred years) that busy thinking became necessary in order to keep pace with everything and everyone around us. My theory is that people with panicky tendencies, such as a quick startle response, and a tendency to dramatize (ahem!), have to *learn* how to adapt to the chaos or they will be constantly nervous, like a rabbit. We all know that a high level of anxiety leads to seemingly random panic attacks. What I learned in studying Buddhism gave me the tools to become a calm evaluator of whatever came my way. I learned to study things or situations objectively, and I developed confidence by making one good decision at a time before going on to the next. Sensible living is so simple, but some of us have to learn how to get back to simple, don't we?

One way to control chaos is to refuse to take it into your life. Remember it is possible to simply *observe* chaos. It's also possible to avoid a lot of life's madness by tuning in instead to the things that are meaningful to you. I finally stopped listening to and watching the news, or any of the transitory goings-on going on. I know I will somehow hear of anything of major importance in world events and politics.

Your job is to become so attuned to your very basic nature that you can see a trigger for a panic attack for what it really is. If the trigger turns out to be a man-eating grizzly, go ahead and hit the adrenaline-accelerator switch and do that lightning-quick disappearing act that your caveperson muscles just made possible. But if the trigger is nothing but light and shadows, don't do anything but enjoy the show. Doesn't that sound simple? All you need to know is: *is it or isn't it the real thing?*

Study of Buddhism will teach you how to concentrate on the things that truly matter. Buddhists think of "things" as transitory, which most are. The belief is that attachment to things creates suffering.[21] By simplifying your life, you may discover the things that make you happy and fulfilled aren't things at all.

Focusing on the essentials will relieve your mind from ideas or situations that make you anxious. The path to simplicity is a process that will affect everything about you, including your thought patterns—which I guess is the point. You will also learn that simplicity is the gateway to creativity.

Many people cannot seem to think of themselves as creative, but *creative* just means having the desire to change and the willingness and means to express change. Someone who is satisfied with the status quo is not likely to be creative. If you're reading this book and you're ready for change, there's one thing you're *not* satisfied with, and that's the status quo. Whenever you *act* to change something—anything!—you are bringing about change with your creative powers.

As you more fully develop your creative side, you will gain increasing confidence, because to a creative person, all things are possible. A creative person can afford the luxury of coming to each new problem or project with nothing but a completely open mind. By embracing your own creativity, you learn that you can *create* a way to live life confidently, serenely, and happily. When you understand this about yourself, you are on a direct flight to recovery.

During the early part of your recovery, you will inevitably take a huge step and learn—by doing—just how creative you can be. At the beginning, as you evaluate the self-made structures that are keeping your fear of fear alive and kicking, you will start to see these structures for what they are—puppet strings controlled by an unseen and out-of-control primitive reflex. When you know this, you can figure out how to cut those strings so you can do your own dance. This requires a huge burst of creativity.

I don't recall just when it happened, but during one of my many desperate moments, I realized I had to be truthful with myself and admit the very scary truth that without puppet strings, there was nothing really reliable to save me during a panic attack. Doing this, I actually made a big step in my recovery. I acknowledged in that moment that *I* was actually all *I* could rely on, and that from then on, I would be working without a net. The high stakes scared me witless at first, but then they liberated me. I was ready to take charge, and I felt lucky to be ready for this turning point when it came.

You have the capacity to be as creative as you will *allow* yourself to be. Anything is possible, and once you cut the strings, believe me, you will continue to want to challenge yourself by being bold and using your new skills creatively.

Compassion

Buddhism teaches loving compassion for all beings. As you learn the value of compassion, you can begin practicing kindness and loving care on yourself. Self-love and self-acceptance are necessary for recovery. Treat yourself as you would any other creature that is enduring pain of any kind. When you recover, you will feel a need to help others overcome their particular pain. You will be able to do so easily because you have learned compassion.

Connectedness

One of the central principles of Buddhism is that all phenomena are related and dependent on everything else in our world—that we are connected to everything on Spaceship Earth. Once you begin to comprehend your organic and spiritual relationships to other beings, and even inanimate objects, you will feel less isolated. Indigenous peoples in the Americas believe that all of nature is sacred.[22]

If you can relate to the critters in your neighborhood, you can also relate to your neighborhood trees and rocks, and this might even offer something to connect with on a scary trip away from the house. It could look something like this: "Say, you are one handsome maple tree. Sugar? I thought so. I'll bet you're related to the maple in my front yard. Here's a picture of her, and that's me underneath. How are you doing? Ah, well, it's been dry up our way too. I'll tell her hello for you when I get back."

Whether or not you want to talk to trees, the more people and things you observe and empathize with by letting them into your circle of awareness, the more connected you will feel. Wherever you go, you will be surrounded by family.

In another way, as you progress with your program, you will begin to see how doing your research and connecting with websites and authors whose words or viewpoints you find helpful also anchor you to the security of a community. A significant part of an agoraphobe's fear is the isolation, the feeling that you're all alone with this torturous condition. Getting *connected* with your world is part of your recovery and will help you grow as a (mostly) fearless person, alive with possibilities.

4

CHANGE YOUR OWN MIND
POSITIVE THINKING
AND VISUALIZATION

Most of us walk around with heads busy as beehives, aware of some thoughts as they come and go but not fully aware of the buzz of mental activity just beneath the surface.

Every once in a while, it's a good idea to stop and ask yourself, *What was I thinking?* After a long spell of unconscious thinking, more often than not, I can trace back my daydreaming at least an hour. In the early days of my recovery, I used to be disappointed at how much of that not-quite-subconscious thinking was dark and negative, or at least not helpful. I, of course, saw the pattern as another example of what a horrible mess I was, which generated further negative thinking.

I have since learned through my work that most people seem to think negative thoughts more often than positive ones. Maybe the average sort of person walking down the sidewalk can afford to do so much negative thinking, but you, my agoraphobic friend, cannot. You will need to achieve a high Positive Thinking Average (PTA) in order to recover. One way to do that is to practice self-love. I invented this stat, so try keeping a record in your journal of your daily PTA. May you bat a thousand.

Each morning when you arrive in the vicinity of a mirror, I want you to look deeply and fondly at that person and say, "I love you." Do this every day. If you are uncomfortable doing so, ask yourself why. Spend some time in this fashion, talking to yourself, and see what it does for you. After I got over the amazing, awkward, uncomfortable feelings, I found it to be a helpful device and a gentle reminder.

Creating your own personal Thought Police is another way to help you direct your thinking toward the sunny side of the street. The Thought Police were first created as a sinister force by George Orwell in his 1949 futuristic novel *Nineteen Eight-Four*, and I've re-created them as a useful force. Use the Thought Police to stop and frisk your brain regularly on suspicion of counterproductive thinking. "Freeze, Brain! This is the Thought Police! Empty your gray matter onto the sidewalk so we can go through your recent thoughts." I learned that the only way I could stop my pattern of negative thinking and reverse my thought patterns was to totally halt myself several times a day to examine my recent thoughts. Include some form of this stop-and-frisk activity in your daily routine until it becomes habit. Civil rights be damned, this recovery business is serious.

One indicator of negative thinking for me was my jaw. Whenever I realized my jaw was particularly tight, I knew something was up, or rather down. So I'd slam the perp up against the brick wall of the alley and say, "All right, punk. Why the tight jaw? What are you hidin', pal? You're on probation, you know. You're not supposed to be possessing those dark alley thoughts. What were you thinking??!!" Or maybe a couple of kindly English bobbies can do the work for you. Remember, it's time to be creative—creativity is the key to your prison cell. Devise things you can do and say to motivate yourself and change your subconscious thinking, as well as raise your PTA.

When I recalled negative thoughts, the best and least complicated advice I could give to myself was simply, "Do the opposite." For example, if I had been thinking, *I'm a hopeless schmuck, and I'll never get out of this dismal, dark scary life,* I didn't have to go very far to get to, *Don't listen to him. I'm actually a loveable person who knows there really is hope, and I can see some light, and I'll reach it by working hard and being positive every day.*

When you have a tune stuck in your head that you're sick of, the best way to change it is to sing a different tune. When you do opposite thinking, make it as vivid as you can. Close your eyes and create a visual image of what you will be thinking that is opposite of what you had been thinking.

Once you establish a routine of checking your thinking and then switching as needed to positive thoughts or stories, your subconscious will be receiving a steady flow of data that will change your response system.

This, again, is how you make changes in neural pathways. I'll bring in Mr. Henry David Thoreau at this time to make the point poetically. This is something I can imagine him processing as he walked round and round Walden Pond: "As a single footstep will not make a path on the earth, so a single thought will not make a pathway in the mind. To make a deep physical path we walk again and again. To make a mental path we must think over and over the kind of thoughts we wish to dominate our minds."[23]

Recall as much as you can of your negative thoughts and try to trace them back. You may be able to break a pattern you aren't consciously aware exists—a pattern that perpetuates negative thoughts. For example, as I pass through my day, I see and hear some things I have a negative or disapproving attitude toward. I know that seeing or hearing one or the other of those negatively charged triggers can get me into a stream of just-below-consciousness negative thinking. I regard negative thinking as a pattern that continues the way inertia works, requiring direct intervention in order to halt it. You will discover particular triggers that you can disarm forever with changed thinking. Presto change-o!

What worked for me was to intervene by creating a storyline for each negative stimulus in order to neutralize it in some way. In other words, turn a threat into something totally harmless through logical argument, or humor, or whatever works best for you. Operate under the belief that if you make up something and say it often enough, it will be true as far as your subconscious is concerned. You already know your subconscious will believe just about anything. For example, a passing thought about, say, being out in a desert presents such a tremendous threat that all the alarms have to go off, triggering a Code 3 Emergency. Thanks a lot.

So let's get busy with some visualizations.

Visualizations

Dreaming while conscious is how I think of visualizations. I can still remember details from the very first time someone led me on a visualization many decades ago. We did it with low lights and music, a relaxing setting. The visual journey required me to be looking down and around as I walked on a path of my choosing, describing details. At one point I was to look far ahead to my particular destination as it grew closer and clearer. There were many details in the session, but the ending was poignant. I was to come upon a dresser whose top drawer contained something left specifically for me. I slowly, cautiously opened the drawer and . . .

I hope you find what's perfect for you in your top drawer. I know you'll find visualization practice helpful. Here's your first one.

Viz 1—The Switchmeister

Let's face it. Your main problem is the adrenaline-firing system in your traitorous brain: the amygdala. It will be easier for you to change the necessary thinking patterns if you can visualize the root of the problem. Create a persona, a figurehead, a being of some sort to be the adrenaline switch operator, code name *Switchmeister*. This could even be someone you know to place in a chair in the inner sanctum of the amygdala beside a big red switch.

The Switchmeister is constantly vigilant, eyes darting about, alert to any and all kinds of "danger," presumably to protect you. Unfortunately, your particular Switchmeister got some bad programming and is now a total klutz, constantly triggering false alarms that are ruining your life.

Go to a quiet place, close your eyes, and create a strong visual image of that character, deep inside the brain, humming with activity. Think of yourself as actually walking through the brain in tunnels and various mysterious chambers until you enter the chamber containing the adrenaline switch and its operator, whomever you have made it out to be. The two of you need to talk. I would say something like this:

"Look, I know it isn't your fault, Amygdala, that you got some jumbled information early in our life so that you aren't always certain when to throw the old adrenaline switch. I admit I probably gave you too many problems to watch out for, but I get the feeling that when in doubt, you go ahead and throw the switch. Listen very carefully. We cannot do that any longer. I am going to send you messages daily telling you to only trigger the alarm when there is genuine physical danger. No more alarms for thoughts I might have or relationship difficulties or blinking fluorescent lights or even loud noises. From now on, you will only throw the switch for things like speeding vehicles or avalanches or dangerous people bearing down on me. Also, any animals with apparent ill intent. Anything we would have to run or jump away from requires an alarm. The rest, not. From now on, if you have questions about a particular threat, consult with the Big Guy, Cortex. I'm not exactly mad at you, but you are making me a nervous wreck and ruining my life with all these false calls to *panic!* so I'm not exactly pleased. I do love you and think this could be the beginning of a beautiful friendship . . . *if you knock off the #%&@!! false alarms!*"

The visit with the Switchmeister (aka amygdala) should take place, if only briefly, every day. Create little stories to say out loud every day to your subconscious system. You could have fun with it—create actual dialogues wherein the Switchmeister makes feeble attempts to explain away the most recent wrongdoing. You could also make your daily messages like memos or sticky-note reminders. Go ahead and yell it out, "I'm going out, dear. Remember, only call if there are genuine emergencies."

I personally feel that you should use humor whenever you can.

Viz 2—The Very Big Trip

This visualization requires a period of quiet alone time. I suggest you do it after you go to bed tonight or a night soon, when you are ready to start this work. I will give you the framework, and you paint the picture. Consider this visualization a work in progress, as you will do your own variations of this many times.

You are alone in a room, waiting for your guide to freedom. The room represents your prison and contains many of the objects, people, and events you have struggled with, and which you will be leaving behind when you become free. Your guide enters the room from a side door and says, "Congratulations! The day you thought would never come has come. You are about to be free. Follow me."

You are led into another room where all is serenely quiet. You see a door on the right wall and a closed curtain on the wall ahead of you. Your guide leads you to the curtain and says, "When you open that curtain, you will see before you your perfect sanctuary. You will see the safe place you have desperately sought all this while. When you open the curtain, you will have an epiphany—a sudden realization that will release you from this prison forever. Here's twenty dollars and a new suit." The guide smiles at the little joke and leaves the way you came in.

Palms sweating (in a good way for once), you pull the drawstring, and there before you is a bright shiny mirror. And there *you* are. Stare with all your might at the person you see in the mirror because that's the *you* that saved your butt, the *you* that had been quietly optimistic all along, the *you* that knew deep down this glorious day would come, the *you* that somehow always figured out how to get you through yet another hard night while you were screaming and being hysterical. This is the *you* you used to be. Actually, you've been there all the time, just heavily overshadowed for a while.

Suddenly, you realize the other you is standing outside, gesturing for you to open the door. You do, and as you step outside, you are bathed in a warm glow. You are experiencing joy you have never felt before; all the weight is gone. This is ecstasy. You race to the other you, and as you embrace, you morph into one. You realize now that you are together again, *you* are all you really need in order to be safe. This is an unprecedented realization. You have become a unified, brave new being, confident in all you do. Therefore the safest place for you to be is inside your own head, a fully equipped survival palace. You are the Taj Mahal.

Now you have to cross a wide-open space to get to the conveyance you will be taking on your Very Big Trip. When you get into the car, bus, carriage, plane, train, or boat, you settle in and begin your amazing journey.

Take this storyline to bed with you and get all the things that need to happen sorted out. Make the entire event as vivid as you can so you can readily get back there. To picture your prison, think of size, colors, sounds, smells, the things there that once terrified you. Describe the guide—clothing, posture, attitude—and the curtain and door in the room. How are you dressed, and is the mirror you exactly the same, or . . . ? What is around you outside? To the right, the left, overhead, and beneath? Describe the open space you have to cross and what you're thinking as you cross. What is your ride, and where are you going? What are your feelings as you begin the trip that will set you free? Describe what you see as you're traveling. Be creative. Talk aloud if it helps you tell the story, and tell it again when you've finished so you make a strong impression on your brain.

As you create your Recovery Program routines, schedule the Very Big Trip visualization about once a week. Change some of the details each time so you go somewhere else or somehow else, thus helping create an adaptability that will be of great help to you on actual trips. Plus you won't get bored. I had a girlfriend once who often said, "The best way to get your own way is to have more than one way." She rarely followed her own advice, I must report, but that doesn't mean being flexible isn't good advice. It is, especially for agoraphobics. Work on varying your regular, safe routines so that each day you encounter something a little different and uncomfortable.

Change such things as how you make the bed, which hand you brush your teeth with, which hand and fingers you use to guide your mouse, the order or way you accomplish a work task, and so forth. Continue to make changes of that sort every day, and record them in your journal. This changing activity helps your brain be plastic and will give you practice for eventually effortlessly doing things that you used to perceive as dangerous.[24] It's all in your head, as they say.

Viz 3—The Normal Minute

Each day, take a small imaginary trip or visit a circumstance that makes you fearful—only, do it the way a "normie" would (someone who is so-called "normal," or at least not agoraphobic, that is). Maybe it's a trip to the store, standing in a long line at the department of motor vehicles, going to a movie, or driving to the next town.

Get into your daydream conveyance (make it a Corvette or Jaguar) and turn on the music, yawn, slowly pull onto the street, closely observe everything on your trip, whistle or sing on your way to wherever you are going, find a little open stretch of road where you can press down the accelerator, have pleasant exchanges with whomever, stop and get something, and go the slow way on your way home, have a smile on your face when you return. Fill in the rest and make it a comfortable, pleasant little experience.

You do not have to make these daily visualizations long, but do make them vivid. And, most importantly, do them with ease, as though you almost didn't have to think about it. Put yourself in the middle of a long line and imagine you have a book in hand that you're enjoying, but you're also chatting with others in line. Think about what you're wearing; that's important. Note all the imaginary scenery on your drive. Make the daily Normal Minute a fun, social experience.

Be sure to treat yourself to at least one of these Normal Minutes per day.

These are the three assigned visualizations. Once you get comfortable creating visualizations, you will easily be able to use the technique to help you get through any difficult circumstances. For example, you have a work-related meeting you have to attend. The problem is, the meeting is at the main office, which is clear across town in an area where you are afraid you will panic. The meeting is in three days, and you are going to perseverate about it anyway, so you might as well do that with positive visualizations.

Prepare carefully whatever you have to present, and then paraphrase it several times a day until you could do that cold. Next, think over and over about the way from the parking area to the office door so you won't have to add that to your anxiety list. Do all these preparations for trips and you will find you need to do less and less each time because your general anxiety level has decreased. You begin to trust yourself.

Every time you start to think fearfully about the dreaded event, imagine yourself in your expensive sports car, driving to the meeting with the window open or the top down and your arm resting in the opening; there are some great tunes on your radio, and you are swaying your head back and forth to the music, happy as a lark. You only need to visualize a short part of the trip each day to get the positive flow going. Make each trip feel as though it were the easiest thing you could possibly be doing. Take the road trip visually several times, using online maps, which are so helpful. Take the trip more than one way in your head until you can see the journey clearly and calmly a number of ways.

Alternatively, the fearful thing you want to visualize may not be a trip, as such. You might want to do a visualization within a building, like a schoolhouse, movie house, mall, or theater. Visualize such things as hanging out in the lobby talking and laughing with friends; sitting on an inside seat, eight seats from the aisle, and loving the clear view because there is no one in front of you; walking down a long, foreboding hallway with the thought that you are in a castle, going to be given a reward for your virtues; or having lunch and a great talk with friends in a very busy, congested place. Your goal is to trick yourself into feeling comfortable about things you have to do that ordinarily make you sick with fear. Make each of these mind trips a happy trip and the real trip will be much easier for you.

Whenever you make a successful actual trip, repeat it soon so that trips once difficult become familiar and comfortable. Record your impressions in your journal.

Please do these visualizations and positive thinking exercises regularly. Neuroscientists have determined that faithful repetition is the key to changing neurological patterns. You may not experience the fruits of your labors immediately; change can slip quietly and almost unnoticed into your thinking process. The point is, positive change occurred for me because I was doing positive work and feeling positive that it would work. Simple as that. If I had kept a regular journal all the time I was actively working on recovering, I know I would have been noticing subtle changes that led to my point of recovery.

I assume you will discover this happening in your journal work. If it occurs to you some morning that you haven't had that feeling of dread for a couple of days, for example, be sure to note it. Every scrap of evidence is helpful in a Recovery Program. Think of it this way: when you begin to hear favorable remarks from people you trust about someone or something you had doubts about, you usually begin to change your thinking to a more positive view. Right? Well?

5

GOOD MED/BAD MED

Ours is an anxious old world. Most of Earth's creatures, from houseflies to Phi Beta Kappas, are wired to be looking over their shoulders. Danger lurks in every kingdom, which doesn't exactly make for utopia, but that's how biology works. It's a dog-eat-dog world, and there are lots of hungry critters out there. Fear of *them* plays a role in the survival of *us*. The difference between humans and supposedly lower animals is that lower animals don't have to take meds to deal with the fear that the possibility of danger creates. Sadly, we of the nervous persuasion can't learn from the animal world that the ideal way to live is to be healthy and strong, and if actual danger presents itself, we'll be prepared to handle it. That way, we don't have to *worry* about danger until the moment something real threatens us. Think of that. How radical.

Level-1 agoraphobes are the complete opposite pole from this animal state. They perseverate about danger, believing the only way to avoid panic attacks is to be constantly on alert. The irony is that not only is hypervigilance the opposite of the best way to be, but also we who think about danger the most seem the least equipped to handle it. An agoraphobe who finally gets blasted by a sneak attack has no idea what to do about it now that it's here. We do all this thinking and preparing and setting up defenses, but when the inevitable occurs, we become totally dysfunctional and incapable of handling our own emergency that we created all by ourselves. At the moment of blastoff, we think and act like complete *idiots*.

The reason we can't do anything, of course, is that there isn't anything to do anything about. Even knowing that we're essentially worrying about nothing doesn't prevent us from being anxious. That sort of fretting is purely behavioral, and a pill ain't going to change it. Thus this book.

But we need to take a moment to talk about the most important thing in the business of mental health: the money.

Anxiety is a surprisingly costly disorder. The National Institute of Mental Health estimates that anxiety disorders cost US taxpayers about $40 billion a year in such things as uninsured medical expenses and lost production because of absences.[25] Add to that figure personal costs resulting from chronic panic attacks, and costs rise even more. Certain parts of the economy benefit from anxiety and mood disorders (the therapy industry and related medical services, for example) but none more than the Big Pharma Industrial Complex and its stockholders. Developing and pushing pills to decrease our anxiety and mood disorders is benefitting that industry to the tune of

$18.4 billion a year.[26] The kicker is that almost all the formulas for tranquilizers were discovered by chance and accident, greatly reducing a company's cost for research and development. Read on.

A Brief History of Tranquilizers

Barbiturates were the first mass-market tranquilizers, going from use by veterinarians soothing savage beasts to use by neurotic humans in a very short period of time in the early 1900s.[27] Scientists discovered by accident that barbituric acid could put dogs to sleep for a short time (without killing them), and one thing rather quickly led to another, resulting in the barbiturate family of sedatives.[28] They were called "barbs" on the street, and the potential for addiction was high. So was the potential for death when combined with alcohol or when consumed in quantity. Barbiturates quickly fell out of favor in the US medical community when benzodiazepines appeared on the market (see below).[29]

A barbiturate formula (phenobarbital) is used as an anticonvulsant and for pain relief, but current barbiturate use for sedation in this country is apparently rare. The powerful drug is used in assisted suicides. Judy Garland, Marilyn Monroe, and Jimi Hendrix were reported to have died from barbiturate overdoses.

Another too-good-to-be-true tranquilizer was Miltown, developed in the mid-1950s through an accidental discovery involving the compound meprobamate putting mice to sleep.[30] The formula was also marketed as Equanil. Miltown and Equanil were fun tranquilizers manufactured by the trainload. They became a miracle answer for mental hospitals where they were used to treat agitated patients, schizophrenic patients in particular.[31] From personal experience, I know these two drugs were like mild knockout drops and could take you from high anxiety to a gentle fog in fifteen minutes. Unfortunately, Miltown had potential for abuse written all over it, and I'm sure doctors were relieved to be able to stop prescribing the highly addictive substance when benzodiazepines were introduced in the form of Librium, discovered by chance in 1960.[32]

From time to time, a new medication with tremendous importance to the public good and company profits is introduced with quite a lot of fanfare. I'm thinking that perhaps the introduction of benzodiazepine to the world went something like this:

> *Ta dah da dun da dun!* sound the trumpets. Saint Benzo appears on the horizon, sunlight glistening off her armor and her sword. Her mighty steed stamps its hooves and tosses its head, the long white mane like an ocean wave. The acclaimed and sainted Pharmacy Rep raises her sword to the sky and slams down her stainless steel visor. Her horse rears, and they begin to charge, leaving a great cloud of dust as they thunder toward the Old Guard, who quickly pack up their chemical formulas and scurry away. The heralded Saint Benzo

is here at last, millions cheering her arrival, as the steed skids to a halt and rears again. Throngs of nervous types crowd around her, crying out, "We are saved! Praise Big Pharma. We are saved! All hail Saint Benzo."

Saint B, as she will come to be known, raises her hand to quiet the masses. "I must continue my Crusade, but I leave behind . . . ," and she beckons a handsome young man on a black Arabian stallion to come out of the crowd and ride up beside her, "Prince Valium, who will represent me and make your lives better." The dark-eyed prince rears his horse and removes his small crown to wave to the masses. And they all lived happily, for a while.

Okay, so nothing is perfect and there really isn't a good med to cure or even treat panic disorder and agoraphobia. Benzodiazepines can, however, used in a very specific way with a very specific timeline, help you get to the point where you can do good work on your Recovery Program. If your level of anxiety is preventing you from getting any recovery work done, a short regimen of a benzo might be just the thing to get you over the hump. The virtue of this family of meds is they provide fairly quick relief from anxiety and are not a risk for use in suicide.[33] The drawback is that after a brief time of use, their therapeutic value comes into question because your body becomes physiologically addicted to the substance.[34] The fact is, when you become addicted and stop taking your particular benzodiazepine, you will suffer withdrawal that feels exactly like unending anxiety.

Isn't that just like life, to be both cruel and ironic at the same time? Here you are taking a pill to relieve anxiety that creates anxiety. I recall when I first realized the anxiety I was feeling was not *my* anxiety. I had been taking Xanax for over a year when it became apparent that my familiar anxiousness that ebbed and flowed over a twenty-four-hour period was no longer around. Instead, I would get this irritating, annoying body buzz every seven hours telling me it was time to take another pill. I felt angry and betrayed when it finally sank in that my new anxiety was being created by a gigantic pharmaceutical company. I really loved my benzos, but I know my recovery was delayed by years because of the addiction trap I was in.

There are numerous YouTube testimonials about negative experiences with benzos. Watch one if you dare.

On the other hand, some people with generalized anxiety can apparently be safely treated long term with benzodiazepine medication so long as they understand the drug will slowly lose effectiveness and they will have to go through a lengthy tapering off to discontinue. These meds are contraindicated for long-term use on people with panic disorder and agoraphobia. If you are currently on a benzodiazepine, you will have to go off it to fully recover. Never having to fear panic attacks again results from what you have learned and done and worked hard to discover, not from what a fickle pill delivers.

Your recovery has to be pure and unadulterated or you won't be able to rely on it. Once you learn enough to *know* that you can free yourself from agoraphobia, your anxiety will lessen significantly, giving you hope. I know it sounds very scary to go off your benzos, but working hard on your Recovery Program will divert you long enough to get over the initial shakiness. Tapering off lessens the symptoms. After that short interlude, you will probably feel more relaxed than when you were taking tranquilizers. I did.

The four benzo meds most often prescribed are Ativan (lorazepam), Klonopin (clonazepam), Prince Valium (diazepam), and Xanax (alprazolam).[35] Another drug in this family, called Halcion, must have had some extra pixie dust on it. I recall thinking Halcion was the best drug I had ever taken in my entire lifetime, by far, when it was prescribed for me in the mid-1980s, and that if only everyone could take it, there would be no more war. Halcion was so good and so appropriately named that I, oops, took a few more than were prescribed. I had to call my shrink two weeks early for a refill and never saw another script for it. Halcion pretty much disappeared from the market shortly after it debuted, viewed by the medical establishment as too fun and unpredictable. Darn.

If you decide to use a benzodiazepine short term to help with your recovery, ask your doctor if Klonopin might be the best choice. I say this because it has the longest life of the family, making it less likely you will feel the daily anxiety of withdrawal.[36] Remember that if you stay on a benzodiazepine too long (one to two months?), you will have to withdraw slowly to minimize the uncomfortable feelings and risk of stroke.[37] Do not go off a benzo without a plan with your doctor. Expect to feel anxious for a while, but that will disappear and be replaced as you progress with your Recovery Program by a naturally relaxed bliss. Truly.

As a side note, my personal experience and opinion are that the tranquilizer called BuSpar will have little if any effect on your anxiety level. It's in a different family, has no sedative effects, and takes quite awhile to engage. I know it does tricky things to your brain, but you're already doing tricky things to your brain with your Recovery Program. You don't need a chemist.

Antidepressants in the Selective Serotonin Reuptake Inhibitor (SSRI) family being used to treat agoraphobia and panic disorder include Prozac, Zoloft, Paxil, and Celexa.[38] I have no experience with SSRI meds, but I must mention a terrifying personal experience with a tricyclic antidepressant, which like SSRIs has been prescribed beyond its antidepressant usage for anxiety. A psychiatrist I was seeing told me tricyclic antidepressants have been effective with anxiety and prescribed me imipramine. I took one in the morning, and by afternoon felt like I'd drunk three pots of coffee. I didn't sleep for a second that night, and by the next day's dosage, I began to feel like I was driving an old rattling Corvette at top speed to the moon. I begged my shrink to stop the experiment after two days, not having the courage to face the "tri" in the three-part horror cycle. I still see tricyclic antidepressants recommended in the literature for panic disorder, but I wouldn't recommend them. The SSRIs are entirely different compounds from tricyclics and don't function in the same way. They affect the flow of neurons from one part of the brain to another. Here is how they are designed to work: when your neuron transmitters release feel-good neurons such as dopamine, some of the material is not taken up by receptors immediately and is reabsorbed for later use. SSRIs act to block the reabsorption so these neurons can give the person an extra boost of positive feelings.[39]

Use of this type of medication may make you feel better in some way, but I advise only short-term use, same as benzos, and a commitment to the nonpharmaceutical solutions in this book. The reason is this: when you take your Very Big Trip and change your life forever, you will only know you are free forever if it was *you* who pulled it off. If it was *you* and *Mr. Med*, how can you trust that for the rest of your life?

This recovery business you're engaging in with *Un-agoraphobic* is equipping you with all you need to be all you need. So, if you think you can only travel if you take meds (by the way, you shouldn't be driving), you won't become un-agoraphobic in my opinion. But then I'm a purist snob. You are doing this work so you can be at ease and free for the rest of your life. The boss says, "Get off the alcohol and meds *first,* and then begin getting ready for a lifetime of traveling and pretty much everything else with ease."

There are homeopathic substances to treat anxiety, including products such as Anxietin, Seredyn, Inositol, and others you can learn about online. GABA is a supplement that may have calming capabilities. Valerian is a time-honored calming herb that can be drunk as tea or taken orally in gelatin capsules. I remember developing a rash after ingesting lots of valerian over several days. The rash went away, but taking even a lot of valerian didn't make my bulletproof anxiety go away. My opinion is that homeopathic solutions are for amateur anxiety as opposed to the major league variety you are on your way to eliminating through this holistic process. So much is available in the realm of herbal remedies that I recommend you consult a naturopathic doctor if you are interested in homeopathic options for overcoming panic attacks. However, again, these are tools that should be only used *temporarily* to ready yourself for significant gain in recovery.

Alcohol is a tempting way to treat anxiety. After all, one little old glass of wine is such a good sedative. So is half a gallon, which is usually the result of medicating anxiety with alcohol. Some people can drink just one glass of wine, but unless you are one of those maddening moderates, do not go there. Alcohol is a depressant that can make you want to give it all up (see chapter 10, "Help for Alcoholics"). As for street drugs, the only ones I know with truly sedative properties are heroin and opium. The benefit of medicating with any of those is that agoraphobia, ironically, would no longer be your major problem. Aside from highly addictive painkillers like Quaaludes and Oxycontin, most other street drugs are stimulants and psychedelics and you would have to be a natural-born fool to stimulate your already overstimulated body.

Mess with psychotropics like Thorazine and Haldol and you'll beg for a panic attack.

Cannabis lies in between uppers and downers because it can both calm and elevate moods. I don't recommend use of marijuana for panic disorder, but I've forgotten why . . . oh, yes, it's partly because the effects can trigger panic attacks, even in people who don't ordinarily experience panic attacks. Believe me, you do not want to experience a panic attack that lasts as long as the cannabis buzz. (I can actually still recall details of a three-hour panic attack in 1972.) Furthermore, you will need to focus at all times on your Recovery Program, and marijuana intoxication does not allow your brain to remain dedicated to one subject for a lengthy period.

Remember?

All of the above is to say that the only way to fully recover from panic disorder is without medication of any kind, though medication can be useful to get you in a good space to work on recovery.

6

EAT (WHILE) NUTS—AND ALSO BERRIES

You are having a terrible time and, although certainly there is much worse suffering in the world, hardly anyone you know in your immediate world has to endure anything like what you are going through. On the other hand, very few in your immediate world have the opportunity to reinvent themselves. That's exactly what you are doing in your recovery as you shape and adopt the ideal way to do nearly everything. The difference is they may not have to reinvent themselves, but you do. Feeling healthy will help you do this work, so let's see what we can do about suiting your diet to your needs. As an added bonus, healthy eating will make you "normal" nutritionally, so that when someone inquires of your well-being, you can respond honestly, "Why, I'm nearly normal, thank you."

I hope you will discover in this chapter much about your relationship to food as well as create an ideal way for you to not only eat but also to be involved with and connected with your food at some level. This entire book is about what you can create and how you can create it, and this is more of the same. Instead of giving you specific recipes, I'll give you ideas about ingredients and some thoughts to follow about diet, nutrition, and gardening as you progress with recovery.

To get to the best of times, though, we first have to overcome the worst of times. Trying to eat well during a period of high anxiety is like trying to enjoy the beautiful sunset while your rowboat is sinking. Needless to say, your concern for, say, getting *all* the B vitamins will be quickly jettisoned when you're in the middle of a catastrophic event. Often we either eat too much of the wrong things or don't eat enough of *anything* while feeling frantic. Unfortunately, as you know, feeling frantic can go on for lengthy periods of time.

Following are suggestions and tips about foods to get you through now while also providing food for thought for your future with food. My hope is you will become a "foodie" and use your creativity to design a diet suited to your needs and desires. The new you is going to be a fascinating and healthy traveler.

These tips for tending to your nutritional needs will be easy and convenient *if* you begin preparing ahead—starting now. If you cook at one level or another at home, I've got recipe and ingredient suggestions, and if you mostly grab something someone else made—either a frozen dinner or a sandwich from a fast food restaurant—I have some hints.

What to Drink

If you are still addicted to coffee, get over it—seriously. Go into rehab or whatever you have to do, because stimulants like caffeine are not doing your nervous nerves any favors. This prohibition includes black tea. *Go decaf!* I gave up coffee at age nineteen because my hand was trembling so badly from anxiety, I could barely get the cup to my lip. Duh . . . And of course you'll need to discontinue cola and other stimulant soft drinks. While everyone around us is knocking down energy drinks, someone has to remain calm, and it may as well be you for a change.

If you're drinking lots of noncaffeine soda and juice drinks, you're still being overstimulated with all the sugar, including high-fructose corn syrup. I'm hoping that as you learn more about how what we put in our bodies affects us, you'll transition to making your own drinks. You can leave a big jug of water in the refrigerator to allow chlorine gas to escape and make it taste better in your pack-around water bottle. I add lemon juice to my regular tap water to make it interesting (1/4 to 1/3 cup for each 2 quarts), and I keep it cold. Lemon has many virtues, among them treating throat infections, indigestion, constipation, strokes, and kidney stones, among other conditions.[40] If your city water is bad, get filters. These have perks beyond your health benefits of plain old water—as you become more and more connected to your universe and to a deeper understanding of big-picture responsibilities and the well-being of all of us, you'll probably stop buying water in plastic and instead start doing political work to improve the world's water systems.

You can replace those evil stimulants you've been consuming with hot or iced herbal teas. I began keeping a jug of Sleepytime tea in the refrigerator as drinking water, figuring that drinking a snooze-inducing tea all day might help take the edge off. It works. Real fruit juices are fine to drink in moderation; just remember that fructose is the baddest of the bad members of the notorious Sugar Gang. High-fructose corn syrup, which you'll find in fruit drinks and many sodas, is the Most Not Wanted by sheriffs in the Public Health Department. It's been found guilty of causing obesity and diabetes as well as annoying the hell out of me when I can't find even one damned jar of jam in the entire gigantic store that doesn't contain it!

So here we are with all these things that are not good for you to ingest, but what are you gonna do, you know? Yes, sugar is a stimulant (as is chocolate) but we can't give up *everything*. We're already suffering too much! *I need the sublime stimulation my sugar/chocolate fix provides,* I hear you cry out. Moderation, my children, will allow continued use of the few things a person's just gotta have. We each possess our little list, and so long as your particular hardwired addiction isn't noticeably impeding your recovery, bon appétit. Artificial sweeteners have so many possible side effects that we're probably better off with honey or raw sugar or deliciously costly maple syrup than with chemical concoctions.[41]

If you require a morning beverage that gives you a kick start, try ginger tea. A strong cup of ginger tea will get your attention with its spicy bite and will be a calming influence on your digestive system. Here's how I make it: Either chop up finely or slice very thinly a piece of fresh ginger root about the size of the first joint of your thumb and put it (the ginger) into boiling water to, essentially, *cook*, by turning to low heat and covering for about ten minutes. More ginger and more time will give you more kick. Fresh-squeezed lime goes well with ginger, and you might like some honey or a little cane sugar as well.

Now let's talk about food. I often felt panicky on arising and would be on the move straightaway, looking for something to distract me enough to stay one step ahead of the Panic Monster. Many times, I didn't eat at all in the morning, wanting to get to my daily routine, be it work or school, because I found the order of structure to be a calming thing. Usually what you can find to eat at work or school is not going to be the best food, so once again, my best advice to you is: don't do what I did. Here are ways to get some fuel to get you underway with your day—be it at work or school or in your recovery room—as you begin the day's work on your Recovery Program.

First Meal

Your blender can be a great ally if you're not capable of or interested in eating solid foods first thing in the day during high-stress times. The following are ingredients for a fruit smoothie/protein drink that resembles a meal. Let's call it the "Survival Smoothie."

1. Liquids: Regular milk, fruit juice, soy milk, and almond milk all provide good nutrients. Almond milk is something you can make at home and keeps much longer than cow's milk. Another attribute of almond milk (it's about the same price as cow's milk if you buy it in stores) is it won't be as digestively distracting as soy or regular milk if you cannot tolerate legumes or lactose. It's best not to use most fruit juices every day because of the sugar thing, although pomegranate juice is highly touted. Yogurt could be the main liquid ingredient and is something else you can make at home when it's time.

2. Fruit: Your favorite fruits can be used to make your drink sweet and pulpy. Bananas, apples, pineapple, pears, and peaches are usually available locally.

3. Supplements: Protein supplements can be divided into three types: soy, whey, and grain/grass/vegetable. Buy these in bulk if you can, for the best price, and remember the legume-lactose advisory.

Of the widely grown and distributed berries, blueberries, strawberries, raspberries, and cranberries top the list with good ingredients and taste that add micronutrients, minerals, and vitamins.[42] I put a tablespoon each of wheat germ and crushed flax seeds in my daily drink. Walnuts and nutritional yeast are other good things to have in liquefied survival food.

A typical quick-and-easy first meal in the United States would be either toast or a bagel with something spread on it or room-temperature cereal with milk and maybe fruit. If you're going this route, try to get whole grain bread and look for multiple grains in cereal. Typical granola cereal has more than one nutritional element going for it. A good store focusing on health foods will carry many varieties of life-sustaining granolas. While you're there, get wheat germ and other nutritional gems to add to your daily cereal, whatever it might be.

Some people like eggs, potatoes, and meat for breakfast. An omelet with browned potatoes and sausage or bacon is a satisfying, heavy breakfast that I wouldn't recommend eating very often. But if you're up for preparing a meal like that, you must be doing pretty well with your Recovery Program.

Here is a way to give your first meal a healing feeling: create a ritual. Make the time into a fairly specific ritual that you can follow every day. One thing that helped me during high-anxiety times was to have structure. When I didn't have work or school to hurry to for a safe routine-filled day, I soon discovered I could subdue my morning anxiety by setting up a meal routine and then other routines during the day. After you observe your routines for your first meal, journal the steps you ordinarily take to prepare whatever it is you're eating, even if it's only pouring cereal into a bowl and milk upon that.

Add some exotic elements to your ritual, such as turning around three times and saying a magic word before opening the refrigerator for the first time of the day. Invent things like that to create a routine that becomes a comforting, structured activity. And it has to be fun. I hope you're okay with talking to the things occupying the fridge. I don't think anything in there, with the possible exception of ice cubes, would *choose* to live in the cold all the time, so take that into consideration. They're doing it for you.

It may help you to turn your entire routine for getting up in the morning and ready for the world into a symbolic, mock-serious ceremony. As soon as you get out of bed, you'll know exactly what to do next and next after that and so on, which will help take away your preoccupation with the daily anxiety. Get creative.

When it finally comes time to eat, take a couple of moments to express gratitude to all the people responsible for food being in front of you. The farmers plant and hope, living with the anxiety of unpredictable weather, not to mention labor and market conditions. Think about the cold, dark milk barn at four on a winter morning and of scorching hot days in the fields, where people spend time planting, weeding, harvesting, and packing our food. Warehouse workers take the heavy load from the fields and sort it and move it—hard and heavy work.

Truckers are gone from home for days on end, blasting their rigs cross-country to provide tropical foods to northern climes. These people all deserve your thoughts, but you will benefit the most by thinking outwardly. Any time you can spend thinking (as opposed to brooding) about something or someone other than yourself will be time well spent.

If your first meal is out of the house, you can create a fabulous ritual. First, you have to rename the place you go for food. (Mine's now called Orbit Pad

13 of the Humantologic Tribe. And whatever you eat is now called what *you* want to call it, and you're eating it in honor to the Voyage of the Third Daughter of Parabolis.)

Okay, now you can eat (if you know the secret word for *spoon*).

Second Meal

If you are able for whatever reason to be doing the Recovery Program during the day, you'll be eating your second meal at home after the morning's merriment, research, and workout. I recommend the very traditional soup, salad, and sandwich—one or all of these at this time of day. My farming and ranching relatives and acquaintances always had their big meal after a morning's work and called it "dinner." It makes sense to eat heavy earlier in the day while you're still somewhat active instead of at night when most folks (even you, probably) slow down.

Before you're ready for a meal, though, think along the lines of things you can make a lot of and keep in the fridge for sandwiches. Egg salad, tuna salad, and hummus come to mind and are easy to eat when you're in the mood. Deli whole meats like turkey and chicken are good for quick sandwiches, and they keep for a while and can be frozen. Real peanut butter and good jam (without high-fructose corn syrup if you can find it) make a classic sandwich that's especially nutritious on whole grain bread. Canned or dried soup might be what you can manage at this point, but start thinking about making your own soups and then freezing some for stormy days (see "Make Soup" below).

If you're eating on the go, do your digestive system a favor and avoid all fried foods. Soup to go is available in most large grocery stores, and in some of those, you'll find salad bars. The best bet for sandwiches includes wraps and burritos that aren't deep fat fried.

Third Meal

Health officials tell us it's good to eat lightly at night so you can digest before going to bed. In order to get at least some food in the evening during freak-out times, I started making vegetable "salads" with rice or noodles of some kind that kept well because of vinegar and a little olive oil. Any finely chopped vegetables blend well with a grain or pasta and will be waiting for you there in the refrigerator to have a few bites in a calm moment. Food like this will provide you something light to eat that will give you good nutrition as well (see "Make Salad" below).

Following is some general advice about improving your diet as you improve your mental health. Remember this, my friend: you may be feeling ambivalent about your diet right now because of the constant struggle with anxiety and panic, and you may not be concerned with living *healthfully*. I don't blame you. I felt the same way—I just didn't care. But, when you recover, you are going to want to *live forever!* You are going to want to do everything at once that you've been unable to because of your restrictions. Get healthy and stay healthy for the glorious days ahead. This is a very important point for you to grasp. You may want to travel a long distance in order to hike to the top of a mountain or to the bottom of a canyon or both. Get healthy so you can live life to the fullest as soon as you recover and so you can be around for a long time to enjoy true freedom.

Dive into research on food, and keep detailed notes in your journal. There are at least two ways you will improve by doing this:

1. Your body functions will calm down while you're researching foods.

2. Eating the right foods will calm your entire physiology.

You can change your metabolic rate by changing what you eat.[43] All in all, your focus on healthy this and healthy that will be drifting into your subconscious, bearing the message that your world is getting generally safer.

Make Snacks

The word *snack* can mean the same as "all I'm going to eat today" to a person maximally stressed with panic and fear. Since you know from history that you can experience a bad spell again, you may as well prepare for the possibility.

The first thing that comes to my mind is trail mix. Make your own with a blend of nuts, sunflower seeds, soy nuts, raisins, chocolate chips, and the like. Use good energy foods to supply your rapidly running motor. Keep ingredients handy to mix up enough for your "hike," even if that hike is just up and down your inner mountains. If you like dried fruit, include some in your emergency supply.

Try, please, to eliminate the usual suspects from your snack pantry: such things as oil-fried chips and pretty much anything that comes in a Mylar bag that you have to pop open. As technology improves, science learns more and more how certain "foods" are actually toxic because of processing and additives. Bad news keeps coming in.[44] I know how tempting it is to have the oil and salt combo of chips. I found I could tickle that particular taste bud with a few stuffed green olives.

I'm sure you've learned the hard way that MSG is quite the sneaky little stimulant.[45] Keep asking restaurants which of their foods contain it and requesting they post it on the menu, and maybe someday they'll eliminate MSG and use creative seasoning instead. Read ingredient lists carefully. Read all about MSG. It's all bad.

Healthy snacks include chopped raw veggies (with dip), handy cheese slices to help with protein and fats to burn, or those cute little yogurt containers to help you get through the day. Remember, though, most commercial fruit yogurt might as well be a milkshake for the sugar content. Try to be an adult and control a heavy sugar habit if you have one. Maintain a couple of bowls around the house with sunflower and pumpkin seeds and nuts like almonds and walnuts. All nuts provide protein, beneficial oils, and nutrients.[46] Good granola with multiple ingredients but not a lot of sugar is a good snack as well as a good breakfast.

Banana bread is easy to make and nutritional, particularly if you use whole grain flour and cut back the sugar. You can toast it for a quick breakfast or eat it late at night as a guilt-free snack.

Don't tell anyone I told you this, but *cookies* can also be a healthful snack. Use whole grain flour, or a combination of flours, and good oil. Eliminate about a third of the sugar called for in the recipe and replace it with applesauce. Include such things as peanut butter and nutritional yeast and oatmeal or pumpkin and—yes, I don't care what your mother says—you can have cookies for breakfast if you made them. Plus, the whole routine of assembling cookies is calming, and then you get to have that amazing smell, and then you get to be popular because you made cookies.

There's a lot to be said on the side of cookies, and I'm just the one to say it.

Make Bread

I'm calling *bread* all things made with flour but not sugar. Pancakes, for example, can be an agoraphobe's secret survival substance. If you make pancakes or hotcakes with whole grains, eggs, good oil, and milk (almond or soy counts), you practically have a complete food. You can add wheat germ and blueberries to make your day. Keep batter around for a few days only, unless it doesn't contain eggs, as in the case of sourdough, which will keep a long time.

Biscuits are easy to mix and bake and can be eaten with peanut butter or jam or both for a nutritious snack. After you get a bit of biscuit baking under your belt, you might want to try the challenge of yeast-leavened bread. Making your own bread can make you feel so connected to your food, you'll have to sit down for a few minutes during the process. You, of course, will spurn bread-making machines and go with tradition by rolling up your sleeves, lining up all the players, and creating a mass of dough that you will be tending for the next two or three hours as though it were your newborn infant. Plus, people always *ooh* and *ahhh* when you show them a delicious nutritious loaf of bread you made.

Once you smell your own yeast, so to speak, you may want to learn even more about this life-sustaining craft so aromatic with tradition and meaning. Bread is considered a basic food by many. The process of baking is a deliberate, absorbing activity, perfect for the panic-stricken mind. If you are homebound for a spell, baking will not only provide you with a comforting series of things to do but will give you a good reason to have company over as well, to admire your new baby.

From that point, you can explore artisanal baking, by creating exotic loaves from recipes around the world. You know what's fun? *Pizza crust.* You, too, can throw a spinning round pizza crust when you make the real dough, with yeast that you let rise. You have to be bold, though, and have high ceilings.

If making your own breads is out at this point, try to get to know the people at your area bakery, if you can get there. When you can, ask about their favorite all-night music, which loaves they like best, where they get their flour, and so forth. Do what you can to learn as much as you can about your neighbors and your daily bread, and you shall rise above panic attacks and agoraphobia.

With bread in hand, can sandwiches be far behind? Sandwiches made with the right ingredients can be all a person would need to eat. If that's all you can do for a while, at least please sit down while you do so. Just think, if you are what you eat, you could be a *Hero*.

Make Soup

Soup is sustenance in the minds of many and is generally thought of as a comfort food. It can also be all you need to eat for a while if you make it well. (Any soup can be run through the blender to make it something you can drink when anxiety is having its way, btw.)

Canned and dried soups will carry the day during these times. As you become more calm, you'll be able to at least contribute something to your daily soup.

Ramen noodles are quick and easy, but a cheap date; you have to supply most of the nutrients. Toss out the little packet in the package and add vegetable bouillon, as well as chicken or beef bouillon if you like, to make noodle soup. Grated aged cheddar cheese tastes great and adds protein. Chopping up and adding vegetables will make it even better for you. I like quick noodles with steamed broccoli and a diced hardboiled egg.

When you emerge from your recent go-around, you can start looking for soup recipes that are not only good for you but delicious as well. Every fully developed agoraphobe should possess a Crock-Pot as part of basic survival gear. To go with that is my Crock-Pot Survival Soup recipe/advisory. If you can, include a quart carton of vegetable soup base and/or one or two cubes of vegetable bouillon as well as beef or chicken bouillon. If you're just using water, let it boil awhile by itself to clear the chlorine.

Lentils (soak them a couple of hours), carrots, potatoes, onions, and broccoli are the ingredients I always use. Meat could be added, and rice could be used along with the lentils. Add a little lemon juice as well as cumin, salt, pepper, garlic, and so forth; put it on high and don't worry your beautiful little head about it, or anything else for that matter. Chile with tomatoes and beans and/or beef is another Crock-Pot favorite. Soup's on—in about four hours. In the meantime, you can focus on your Recovery Program, making progress as your space fills with the classic, healing, nurturing smell of soup.

Make Salad

To many Westerners, *salad* means something with lettuce that you can play with while you're waiting to eat; mostly, it means it's time to eat your greens. But salad can take many forms and, done properly, can be a complete meal. If you're at the point of being able to have a meal with a salad, you must be about ready to graduate.

Until then, though, you don't have to *make* a salad to have a salad. The hassle of cleaning and cutting up and putting together a bunch of ingredients can be too much some days (or weeks or months), and can even be dangerous. Shaky hand holds a sharp paring knife blade very near other shaky hand, which holds down an unsteady pepper. Sound safe to you? I recall a friend standing in my kitchen one day watching me cut an onion with my anxiety trembles. She said, "Watching you do that makes me nervous." To which I responded, "How do you think it makes me feel?"

One way to get your greens is to keep a bag of green lettuce or spinach open a little in the fridge so you can reach in and rip off a piece as you pass. A healthy friend of mine keeps a lidded jar in the refrigerator with bite-size pieces of carrots, celery, radishes, cauliflower, and other salad ingredients so she can grab a handful off and on throughout the day. Try that, if salad prep is in your grasp. Short of that, sliced carrots (place your palm on top of the back of the blade and press down with both hands please) in a bowl of water can give you something healthy to snack on; you can dip them like chips in a yogurt dip.

Grain salads can be easy to put together and will remain viable in a refrigerator container for a while, particularly if you use vinegar along with oil. Try brown rice with finely chopped veggies and seasoned vinegar, with a little olive oil. It's helpful knowing this marinated treat is there when you need it. Many cooked grains make an easy and healthful base for refrigerator bowl salads, including various kinds of rice, wheat berries, bulgur, couscous, millet, and quinoa. As you do your journal studies on all these new foods, you'll learn that history of grains is the history of the world.

Potato salad is easy to make and provides plenty of protein when it contains hard-boiled eggs.

If you can lay your hands on some yogurt, bananas, apples, and any other kinds of fruit, you will have a nice refrigerator salad bowl to dip into for a few days. Adding a bit of anise makes fruit salad killer. The thing about fruit, though, is fructose. Too much can add to your "sugar deposits," so don't make this into meals, just occasional salads.

Keeping fresh greens around is a challenge to a highly stressed agoraphobe, for whom the produce section of the closest grocery store might as well be on the moon. Welcome to the world of sprouts for in-your-face protein, vitamins, and minerals. You can buy sprouts very fresh if you can get to a store that supports a fairly local industry, but I urge you to grow them at home. Get seeds at your area bulk foods store or through the mail. Procure some nylon window screen and you can, with rubber bands or canning lids, make sprout farms out of any quart-size or larger jar. Cheesecloth will work as a strainer; it's just so messy when seeds and sprouts get caught in it.

The procedure for making sprouts does not require the expertise for, say, assembling something that could fly into outer space. Mindfulness of inner space, on the other hand, would be the perfect trait for a sprout farmer to possess. Soak your seeds overnight in the jar with the screen or mesh in place as a lid. Pour that water out the next morning, and refill and pour out a couple times before setting the jar upside-down to drain awhile before laying it on its side. I usually rinse mine two or three times during the day to keep them fresh. You can increase chlorophyll content by putting them in sunlight part of the day, but my experience is that a bitter flavor results.

My suggestion for the best sprouts in your jar garden is a combination of alfalfa, lentil, and mung. I started adding radish seeds for the zest. Buy only the seeds intended for sprouts for human consumption. Every morning when you get to the kitchen, your little sprouts will have grown bigger through the night. After only three to five days of this . . . ta-da! You're a proud farmer. As with every other subject you encounter in your recovery, learn all you can about sprouting so you could pass a quiz on the subject.

Try to make area farmers' markets part of your community and get as much food there as you're able, perhaps with the assistance of a neighbor or friend. Many food growers at a typical market grow without poisons and will advertise themselves that way when they are certified. Area meat producers are showing up at community markets with organic products they'll be happy to tell you about. Community market people are fun to talk with. You'll find bread there.

I hope that as you learn, you will realize the value of using certified organic foods as much as possible. There are issues of cost and availability, of course, but my argument is that organic foods benefit the panicky, agoraphobic person in two important ways:

1. There is convincing evidence that some food additives, food preservatives, and some pesticides and herbicides can cause hyperactivity and agitation. Artificial food colors and flavors particularly are suspect for causing anxious-like symptoms. Poison, government approved or not, is probably not the best thing for your emotional well-being. See above.

2. The second reason is spiritual in nature, a case for healing through conscientious eating—making a connection with your food community, which is very possible when you go organic, particularly when you grow it or at least buy local organic.

Surviving Survival

As you pull out of your nosedive and begin to regain your composure, let's talk about viewing food and diet holistically—as you are viewing everything throughout your recovery work, learning how the part affects the whole.

A way to do this is through research. List in your journal the categories of things you eat—for example, "Flour, dairy, cereals, beef, poultry, vegetables, greens, sugar," and so forth. After that, list foods you regularly eat from each category, in approximate order of frequency. Your job now is to *optimize* each of those foods, by doing research into, for example, the best flour(s) for you. Whole wheat flour is scored highly, but if gluten sensitivity is a problem, you get to turn the problem into an adventure by learning about all the other flours you can use for bread, cakes, and whatever you want to bake. Look for spelt flour in your local bulk foods store if you're sensitive to wheat. The flour from this ancient predecessor to wheat is quite flavorful.

Is cow's milk working for you? I drink almond milk now and love it. Look at the options and alternatives for each food you eat. Which is the optimum vegetable? For me it's broccoli, best by a head. Which kinds of meat benefit your body most, and how does your body handle digesting meat? Is poultry a good option?

Connection is an integral part of your recovery, as you've been discovering along the way. Strengthening or initiating connections between you and your environment, your friends and relatives, your automatic-response system, your education sources, connecting to *everything that is your life* is critical to your freedom. *Getting to know about* is pretty much the same as *getting familiar with*. The more you become familiar with yourself and your world, the fewer things the old fight-or-flight system has to be alert to. Your community of familiar things and feelings will continue to grow as you continue your Recovery Program. You're learning why a strong connection to your food is an important part of the big picture.

Gardening

The best way to learn about ingredients is to grow them yourself. Gardening at any level is the ultimate connection to your food and can be done anywhere—from your yard to your porch and windows to a glass jar or two you keep near the kitchen sink.

I hope you will find a way to incorporate gardening in your new life. If you cannot grow where you are, learn about community gardens. If there is not a place you can travel to in order to garden, see if there's a community food-buying club. These clubs usually make arrangements with local growers to provide what members ask for. Doing this would at least give you a sense of food community and launch you into a fascinating new world of small-farm production.

7

CALL IN THE PROS
THERAPEUTIC AND LEGAL HELP

If you haven't already in your journey had to engage professional legal and/or therapeutic assistance, you should learn how now. I'll reveal some how-tos with lawyers below, but first I'll help demystify the professional field of personal therapy.

The Shrinks

If you can afford to see a psychotherapist, start doing so at once. If you can only afford a therapist for a short period of time, schedule it so the therapy is of greatest benefit to your Recovery Program. A therapist who specializes in panic disorder and agoraphobia will probably help you recover more quickly than you can with this book alone, but if you cannot afford therapy, I offer some suggestions at the end of this chapter.

A trip through the Yellow Pages or online under "counselors" or "mental health" will reveal what is available in your area. The first thing you will notice is lots of initials; mental health people love their initials. When I worked in mental health, I didn't have any pertinent initials (I'm an English major), so I convinced the phone list coordinator to add the letters EIEIO after my name. Below are some other of the initials I know of that you may associate with mental health.

> **MD psychiatry:** A psychiatrist is a medical doctor who completed medical school and went on to specialize in psychiatry.

> **LCSW:** Licensed clinical social worker. Has advanced degree in social work and has done hundreds of hours of clinically supervised therapy to get licensed to do therapy.

> **MSW:** Master's degree in social work and hundreds of hours of supervised therapy.

> **MA psychology:** Master's degree in psychology, with supervised therapy training.

> **PhD psychology:** Two or more years of school beyond a master's degree plus a thesis in some specialized area of mental health, as well as supervised therapy training. People with these two degrees are called "psychologists." (Psychologist is maddeningly often confused with psychiatrist.)

RN psychiatry: A psychiatric nurse is a registered nurse who has done supervised therapy training and can prescribe psychotropic drugs.

LCPC: Licensed clinical professional counselor. This license is required in most states and involves a specified number of hours of therapy training.

LAC: Licensed addiction counselor. Most states require this license for a person to set up practice in addiction counseling.

MAC: Master's degree in addiction counseling, a degree program requiring a number of hours of supervised training.

EDD: Doctorate in educational counseling. This degree beyond a master's is achieved through hundreds of hours of class and practical experience in school counseling.

Some therapists wanting more initials will include also the initials of a club they belong to, for example ACSW (Academy of Certified Social Workers), or the initials of a technique they use, like DBT (Dialectical Behavioral Therapy). You might see a therapist dripping with initials—LCSW, MSW, ACSM, DBT— and now you can begin to sort out what they mean. Additionally, many therapists will list their specialties, which will help narrow your search.

Call each promising therapist or therapy office and ask what techniques they use to treat agoraphobia. At this time, or at an initial consult, you could tell a prospective therapist about your goals and plans, and your use of this book. Recovery from agoraphobia depends partly on intuition, so let your intuition guide you in selecting a therapist. Do not judge a book by its cover (or initials or bling); let the book speak to you. Once you feel comfortable and confident in a particular choice, let the therapist know more about your Recovery Program and the work you have done so far.

If you cannot afford a private practice therapist, call your community mental health center to see if you qualify for help there. Most community centers require insurance or Medicaid, but sometimes they can take clients under specially funded programs. Mental health centers often have interns who need therapy hours. Ask about that. If there is a college or university in your area offering counseling degrees, call to see if they offer sessions with graduate student therapists. A community health clinic with a sliding-scale fee structure will sometimes have a licensed social worker on staff who can do therapy.

If none of that works out, call a counseling service that seems to have several therapists and ask about getting a panic disorder/agoraphobia therapy group going. Mental health is cheaper by the dozen.

Because I have vast experience with therapists and therapy, I feel qualified to tell you that therapy is not magic. The healing of you will depend much more on what *you* do than what the therapist does. The act of hearing yourself tell somebody else what you are up to is a significant part of the therapy process. A good therapist will help you redirect your thinking as well as help you focus on necessities. Even if you don't find the ideal arrangement, I promise you will benefit greatly from whatever form of therapy you can arrange. Remember, you're not *crazy*; you just need a *thinking consultant*.

You might also want to join or start a peer support group as outlined in chapter 9, "Peer Support Groups." Even though a peer support group wouldn't be traditional therapy, nor should it be used in that way, starting or joining such a group offers tremendous therapeutic benefits. Additionally, tap in to the grassroots action in any of the agoraphobia support forums for some group comfort and a sense of belonging. Searching or initiating a conversation topic on therapy in one of these online groups might yield some good tips as well.

I also recommend that you investigate biofeedback as a therapy and as a tool you can use when your anxiety level soars. Biofeedback has to do with monitoring and having an influence on your body functions, such as heart and pulse rates, breathing rates, muscle tension, and so forth. It would be best to do biofeedback with a professional, but in the meantime, you will find some useful suggestions in the usual places. Mindfulness is a big part of biofeedback.

If you're absolutely broke, or cannot get out of the house, another way (in addition to using this book) to work on yourself is through cognitive behavioral therapy. CBT is a therapy technique that places the workload on the client, asking you to understand that your viewpoint affects your mood. CBT helps you find ways to change your thinking by training yourself to think differently about a given thing, or things. An online search will quickly lead you to some suggestions about how to teach yourself CBT techniques.

The Lawyers

There may be any number of reasons your disability requires legal assistance. Mercy knows the troubles anxiety disorder can create, ranging from alcohol-related incidents to legal debt problems. If you cannot afford a private attorney for your legal problems, Legal Aid may come to your rescue. The volunteer organization is becoming more and more muscular even in smaller communities. Look to Legal Aid for at least directions. If your agoraphobia-related legal troubles are, shall we say, of a more serious nature, I'm sure you already know about the public defenders office.

If your condition is severe enough to prevent you from supporting yourself through work and if you are an adult citizen of the United States, you most likely qualify for disability income through the Social Security Administration. What follows is information about applying for the program and about finding an attorney to assist you.

"Panic attack with agoraphobia" is listed as a "seriously disabling mental illness" (SDMI) in the *Diagnostic and Statistical Manual of Mental Disorders: DSM-5*.[47] This is the big book that medical and legal communities use to define, categorize, and identify mental illnesses. Having your disorder listed is of tremendous help if you decide to apply for assistance.

A person, as you well know, can go from having a normal life to having a panic attack and then another and end up living in a nightmare of near constant panicky feelings. Can you work under these conditions? I couldn't keep my job when that was happening to me.

When I lost a dream job because of a recurrence of panic attacks, I was saved from homelessness by Social Security disability income. The Uncle Sam System really came true and made it possible for me to at least live indoors and eat until I recovered and was able to start working again. Imagine the agony of a homeless agoraphobic person.

Look in the Yellow Pages for an attorney who specializes in disability cases (usually listed in the categories "Social Security" or "disability"). Most of that category of lawyers will interview you to determine if you have a qualifying disability. Take a good definition of agoraphobia with you as well as documentation of when you had to quit working and how your condition has affected your ability to work.

Before the interview begins, ask about fees. Most disability attorneys will represent you for a percentage of the back pay, meaning you probably won't have to pay any up-front fees. Back pay amount is determined by the date you were no longer able to work through the date you begin receiving disability payments. The figure is typically several thousand dollars for someone who had been working regularly.

If an attorney decides to represent you, she has to have a good feeling about your chances because she's risking not getting paid for her work. Give her some background and medical information on agoraphobia as well as your brief personal history as it pertains to developing agoraphobia. You can use information from this book as well as material obtained online. Help your attorney as much as you can because the more evidence she has, the more likely you will prevail. Get written testimony from the appropriate people. For example, ask your boss or supervisor to write a letter about your reason for quitting. If friends or relatives have to do things for you because you cannot, ask them to write statements to that effect. If you have seen a therapist about agoraphobia, those notes can be used as evidence.

Do not be discouraged if you are denied after your first application; many people with disabilities are turned down at this point and have the option of appealing the decision. Fill out and file an appeal— that will get you in front of a federal judge who determines disability cases. Keep in mind at all times that you are there to make the judge understand that your disability prevents you from being able to work enough to support yourself. The protocol is to have you receive a mental health evaluation before the hearing. This is an opportunity to supply the mental health professional who will be evaluating you with anecdotal as well as written evidence of the severity of agoraphobia. We have to educate people in the right places about the condition or we won't get the help we need.

You will probably be asked to testify at your hearing, so if speaking in front of people is a problem, do some rehearsing. There won't be more than five or six people, including you and your lawyer. Ask your attorney what kinds of questions you will likely be asked so you can go in fully prepared to make your case. If you have someone you can role-play with, ask your lawyer to word some questions for you so you can rehearse enough to get you through it. Anxiety is, after all, the reason you are having a hearing. You don't want to be disguising the fact that you have panicky symptoms. Be yourself.

One of the benefits of receiving Social Security disability is you also receive Medicaid, which qualifies you for help with medical services, including mental health therapy with counselors who can and will accept Medicaid clients. (Some don't, as Medicaid doesn't pay professionals as well as private pay and some other insurance programs do.) Social Security will likely review your case in some way in a few years, asking for evidence that you are still medically disabled. Let us presume this will be a moot issue for you because with the help of *Un-agoraphobic*, you'll be happily working again long before that time.

8

MANAGE YOUR RELATIONSHIPS

As a fully developed agoraphobe, you perform many balancing acts, among which maintaining relationships is the most difficult. Sometimes you cannot get to places on time, or at all, and you can't always take care of all your responsibilities, which throws most of your relationships out of balance.

In a perfect world, others would take into account your rather severe but temporary disability and make other arrangements until you are able to function fully again. If you had broken your pelvis, putting you in a body cast that made you walk like a zombie, people would jump up to open doors and get chairs and meals and do your work for you with smiles on their faces. You the agoraphobe, however, learn that most people are vaguely suspicious about your condition (or whatever it is) and give you the feeling they think you could really do whatever it is if you really wanted to.

This prevalent cynicism, coupled with the embarrassing difficulty of explaining our restrictions (when we don't even understand them ourselves), can lead a person disabled by agoraphobia to be sneaky and deceitful. For example, I twice paid someone else to write while I took credit for newspaper stories I was assigned to do. I had no choice. They were both covering long events in crowded buildings when I wasn't doing very well at all—situations that would without a doubt have triggered a panic attack. I also outright lied, many times, to cover for my restrictions. You are on a mission to heal yourself, but you cannot educate the entire planet about your mental illness just now.

Who They Are

Whether you have a marriage or other long-term partnership, children or other family in your household, or are dating, you will *all* probably have to make adjustments in lifestyles because of your agoraphobia. Your recovery will proceed best if you can maintain solid relationships despite having to ask for concessions or assistance in many, often humiliating, ways. Here is my view of your prospects for help from various kinds of people we spend a lot of time around, followed by some suggestions on how to deal with these so-called normal people, the "normies."

Spouse/Partner

Maaaybe relying on your live-in for "agoracare" will work, but be advised that doing so can be hazardous to relationships. It could certainly change the dynamics. When you get down to it, only dead saints really want to devote themselves to totally caring for someone else—even a spouse, especially one who appears pretty normal. Be *very* honest with one another on this issue. The partner should ask herself, "How much help do you need, and how much am I willing to provide day after day?" I hope you never have a housebound faze, but if you do, try relying on friends to help with some of your needs. Getting a spouse or partner to understand and accept your condition will give you plenty to do. There is always, of course, the possibility of living with a live saint. (Don't you wish.)

Kids

Be very careful here because it is too easy to use children for security. If you are a single parent having a frantic, panicky day, and your kid or kids are about to leave for school, it might be tempting to ask one to stay home to keep you company. A lot of kids might like a vacation from school, but it's never going to be a good idea for your children to feel like they have to be your caretakers. I have more advice later on for agoraphobes with kids, but for now, remember that engaging in serious play with kids is one of life's best diversions, so you have that as a double benefit. Do a lot of that.

Family

A supportive parent or sibling can be a blessing for a suffering progeny, but ask that you be allowed to control the assistance. You know how you feel about pressure, and we all know that well-meaning parents can scare the horses. Work it out so no one feels either used or abused, and then enjoy whatever familial help you can get.

Bosses

I wish I had been more open with some of my bosses; others I just couldn't have approached. As it was, I had to make a lot of lame excuses as well as anger some people in several places I worked over the years because of my restrictions. I began my adult working life as a newspaper reporter and was, luckily, promoted to an editor position after two years. Editors sit at desks and don't have to travel. Before that, I had turned down some out-of-town reporting work because of agoraphobia, but I knew I couldn't continue to dodge assignments. Had I, however, been able to go to my boss after I'd proven myself and told him of my problem, I think he would have been understanding and assigned me only to stories I could cover. All bosses are different, but I am certain my work life starting as a teen would have been easier had it been possible to work it out with some of my employers to be able to somewhat control how I had to do my duties and where I had to perform them.

Here is the problem with *not* informing your boss: more than likely, you will miss work and be late to work as well as have to suddenly leave work from time to time because of gripping fear and panic attacks. Better your boss knows what's up than to think of you as a poor worker and either fire you or not write you a good recommendation. Here's the problem *with* informing your boss: I wouldn't blame an employer for not wanting to staff someone who couldn't necessarily be depended on to be at work when needed. If you suspect your boss is that kind and you can cover up your panic attacks for now, do so. That will be extra incentive to make this program work for you.

Teachers

The same sort of advice that goes for bosses goes for teachers, except that teachers can't fire you. They can, however, drop your grade in a class for excessive absence or lateness. If you think your restrictions might adversely affect your relationship with a teacher and therefore your grade, by all means, present the whole agoraphobia education package. Here I am telling you to do something I never did, but I know people are generally more hip to mental illness now than back in my stone age. A good teacher could be very helpful to you, so don't hesitate to approach faculty if you need special considerations.

Friends and Dating

A true friend wants to know you and understand you and be with you through hard times. If you're lucky enough to have a true friend or two, you have support. If you want to continue to have these true friends in your life, I advise you to let *them* figure out how to help you. When you get to the point of telling them your story because you need their help and understanding, allow them to be creative in assisting you so they won't feel used in any way. Did you read Mark Twain's *The Adventures of Tom Sawyer*? Do you remember the episode where Tom made painting a fence seem so appealing that his pals fought over who would get the paintbrush first?[48] I'm not exactly saying you should do that with your friends, but talk with your confidants often and let them know what you're up to so they feel informed but not guilty or obligated. (See more about friends in chapter 11, "The Very Big Trip."

If you have recently started dating someone, you would be foolish to use this person to assist with your problem. The initial rush of endorphins might be all the help you need, though. See below.

How to Deal with Them
Spouse/Partner

If you are in a marriage or something similar and have recently become agoraphobic or need to finally reveal your deep dark secret, you are probably scared to death. It is considered normal for partners to be dependent on one another, but people with agoraphobia sometimes feel it's a matter of life and death to stay connected to their partner. The notion of losing that safety net can trigger a string of panic attacks. The terrifying prospect of losing a relationship is something everyone with agoraphobia must at least think about, if not prepare for. (Please don't take this the wrong way, but would *you* want to live with the agoraphobic you?) Agoraphobic people are generally hypersensitive to the trauma of loss, an effect that should be studied and talked about more. We don't want to be pessimistic, but we also want to be prepared so we don't crash.

Let us consider a worst-case scenario wherein panicky feelings have made you so dependent on your partner that you suffer severe anxiety in the person's absence and cannot go anywhere without him or her. Your partner (designated X so you can think of X as a problem to solve, not a lopped-off persona) has told you she or he cannot continue living this role of constant nurse, and a divorce is in the works. X is going to be moving out of the house and ending the relationship in two weeks if you don't return to normal.

If you are in circumstances like these, start preparing now for the possibility that you will be alone in the very near future. Getting this sudden mandate has actually made your anxiety worse, so the prospect of returning to normal in two weeks seems unlikely. Negotiation should be your first move, asking X to do couples counseling with you or to at least read online information about your condition (as well as this book). Perhaps X would agree to watch some YouTube testimonials from sufferers of agoraphobia in order to comprehend the realities of your condition. If you are seeing a therapist, ask X to sit in on a session. Your therapist can clinically explain the magnitude and manifestations of your disorder better than you can.

After you have revealed everything you know about agoraphobia and have answered all your partner's questions, obviously a decision will be made. I recommend you control the timing as much as possible so you don't become a basket case waiting to hear what your partner is going to do. I think it is best for both of you that you honor the decision and go forward accordingly. Begging or trying to change the decision in any way is the worst thing you could do. My advice is to prepare two courses of action and to take the one determined by your partner.

Soon after your initial announcement, say something along these lines: "I am working on overcoming agoraphobia, and I know in my heart I'll be normal again someday, but I can't promise you anything. If we have to separate because of this, I'll understand. You have to take care of yourself. The truth is, I don't know if I could do this thing I'm asking you to do, were our roles reversed. I would prefer that we stay together, but if we have to part, I want it to be in the best possible way, with no ill feelings." You might be tempted to say something about "getting together again when I recover." I wouldn't, but that's just me. I don't like tenuous relationships. Sometimes it's truly best to just move on. Sometimes a relationship is instead a "needinship." (Hey, I just made up a word.)

If your efforts fail to keep the relationship going, prepare for the worst possible outcome, which we agoraphobes are pretty much world-class at doing, at least in our imaginations. By that, I don't mean for you to be pessimistic, just realistic. With the threat of a panic attack, even in the face of our best-laid plans, putting certain things into play for possible use later is a common-sense thing for an agoraphobic person to do. Here are some suggestions to help you survive separation:

1. Work particularly hard on your Recovery Program during the ordeal to help you remain calm and focused as well as hopeful.

2. Plan to either have a friend come over and maybe even spend the night on the day X moves out, or go to a friend or relative's house. Make this a good time to start having friends over for tea or lunch, something to look forward to.

3. Plan some remodeling, even if it's only painting, to give you something to do as well as put your stamp on the place. Change the furniture around, particularly the bed. On the other hand, you may be the one moving. If you're okay with a new place, then you're on a roll to thriving through this. If you're not okay with it, fasten your seat belt and learn what you can from an exceedingly hard time. You will survive because you just read this sentence; therefore, you are on your way to recovery.

4. Look ahead in your community calendars for activities or events you could attend around the time separation will occur. With a friend, even better.

5. Start something new that you could realistically do on a regular basis, like join a yoga group that's in your territory, or take an art class. Be around

happy, interesting people. Book reading groups are good social opportunities.

6. Try volunteering at some place accessible to you. I recommend nursing homes as places where you would be looked on with appreciation and admiration. Doing good work for others will raise your self-confidence and lower your anxiety.

7. If a new relationship possibility suddenly appears, proceed with extreme caution. (See "Friends and Dating" below.)

8. This would be the perfect time to begin a peer support group if you have the energy (see chapter 9, "Peer Support Groups").

If your partner decides to stay with you, there are still many things to consider. The first is *how* to involve your partner in your Recovery Program. Here is my advisory: If your partner gets heavily involved in your program, he or she might begin to develop expectations—"How soon?" for example—which may not match your own. Differing expectations are already plentiful in most relationships, so be certain you want to risk adding another by having your partner work closely with you on your program. On the other hand, you might be partnered up with an intuitive angel who will always do the right thing for you. If so, lucky you.

I recommend that if your partner wants to help with your recovery, assign specific research that will save you the time of hunting. If your partner doesn't want to do any actual work, set aside a time each day or every few days that the two of you can sit down and review what you've learned and been doing. Always keep in mind that you are doing this recovery work for yourself first, with the knowledge that others may benefit when you recover and become free.

Kids

Agoraphobic parents, especially single parents, have a very difficult life. Raising children is stressful for all parents, but "normies" cannot know how terribly stressful parenting is for someone who cannot at this point in time do some of the basic things society demands, like getting your kids to school and school activities and getting yourself to teacher conferences. Life is exceedingly unfair for you as a single parent who cannot travel or work and whose children need more than you think you have to give. The first thing you need to do is pour all your pride into a blender, drink, and swallow it. The next thing to do is ask for help.

When I was bound up by agoraphobia and had to occasionally ask someone for help, I felt ashamed and embarrassed. Finally, I recalled that whenever someone reveals to me they have a difficult problem and need my help, I am almost always honored that the person respects me enough to ask. I usually go out of my way to do what I can, and afterward, I feel good about myself and happy that I was able to assist. Now that I have maneuvered this concept into my consciousness, I always feel like I am doing someone a favor when I ask for help. Try that.

If you don't have enough income to keep the family going, it is your duty to your children, as well as yourself, to apply for assistance from government programs. Remember that we all pay taxes to provide for people like agoraphobic parents when they need the help. Call your community public assistance office and find out what programs you qualify for that will help your children with food and medical care. Your kids need a lot at a time when you feel like you are barely able to take care of yourself, and *everyone* with agoraphobia understands your special problem. You have to protect them, love and nurture them, but also allow them freedom to grow, all the while struggling with your debilitating, restricting condition.

Bless you for all you are doing. You will be a super advocate for school support issues when you recover—as well as a candidate for sainthood and maybe even school board.

Remember, you *will* get back on your feet and function in society again. Let us keep things in perspective, after all. The entire amount of help you might receive during this time probably won't amount to as much as it costs to outfit one soldier for warfare (almost $18,000).[49] Here you are living the life of a combat soldier, but you didn't even get a protective uniform or a gun to use on the enemy.

Following are some suggestions for ways you can not only survive but also thrive during your experience as an agoraphobic parent.

Inform Your Children

A hard question for an agoraphobic parent is how and when to tell children about your condition. The time is always now. Children are very sensitive to odd behaviors, and if you have been having excessive anxiety and some panicky displays in the house, please talk to them.

An approach for kids under ten who need an explanation that won't alarm or frighten them is to use benign-sounding phrases and examples. Since all kids understand the startle response (how the body reacts to a loud noise or unexpected stimulus), explain that your startle reflex gets triggered easily, and for now, you have to avoid places or conditions that startle you. The story you use to explain yourself should be similar enough to the real thing so you can morph it into reality as time passes. Inform them that you are seeing a doctor for treatment and that you will be well again fairly soon—you're just not sure when. Don't make a big deal about it for young kids; that's my advice. If they have questions, answer them simply, but don't feel you have to elaborate if they aren't asking.

Kids over ten deserve a more scientific explanation. Give them a way to study simple brain functioning that shows how the amygdala can trigger a startle response that can lead to a panic attack. Try to keep them focused on the scientific aspects of agoraphobia instead of the vague emotional issues, which could be disturbing to young minds. For certain, help them understand that it's not a defective gene they could inherit. Tell them that what you have is a condition, like a broken arm, that will heal. Suggested mono-logue: "It's the result of a faulty signal in my sub-conscious that makes me hypervigilant about panic attacks, which means being just kind of nervous. I'm retraining my brain to change the signal so I won't be startled so easily any longer." Make it real, but not threatening. Perhaps one of your children will grow up to be a brain scientist because of you.

Appearing "Normal"

Your next job after informing your children is to appear as much as possible like a "normal" parent. I remember how badly I felt for kids who had a parent who was odd or peculiar in some way. They seemed embarrassed about their family and never invited any-one to come over. Do not make your child suffer in this way by being or seeming like one of those wacko parents. Encourage your kids to have friends over after school and for sleepovers so they can see how "nor-mal" you are. Fuss over your kids' friends and connect with their parents to demonstrate that, aside from the fact that you never show up at games or school activi-ties, you really do care. If you can have a friend or two of your child's over on weekends, or occasionally after school, those parents will probably show their grati-tude by helping do things you cannot manage just yet.

Be creative in your search for help that will make your kids' routines as normal as possible. For exam-ple, if you know people who go to the movies or the mall a lot, ask if they could take your kids along a time or two. If there is someone in your neighborhood who shops regularly, ask if she could pick up school basics for you. If you know an artist, that person might enjoy taking your kids once in a while for art play. I enjoy having one or two friends' kids in my pottery studio. (I've observed that when kids make art and play with clay, they get magically quiet and focused. We could all learn from them.)

There is a risk in reaching out to others too much, but utilize help as much as you can without causing damage. Be sensitive to this. If someone starts showing hesitancy to pitch in, call on someone else for a while. Do your best to keep all your friendships intact. If you can do some kid-sitting or cooking or other deeds for friends, you can balance the scales.

Stopping the Cycle

The mental health of our children should be our primary concern as parents. When this storm has passed and you have returned to good mental health, you will be trying to learn what the effects have been on your kids. If your children seem excessively nervous or distracted, check it out with them and work with your school counselor to get a handle on it. Above all, your imperative duty to each child is to stop the anxiety cycle at you. If you keep your kids informed about your anxiety problem honestly, openly, and fearlessly, *you probably will not pass anxiety along to your children.* Breaking the cycle is a medal-worthy thing to do.

Transportation Dilemma

If your arrangement with your spouse does not cover taking the kids to almost everything alone, you will need to get help from others. If you have had frank disclosure with your spouse about your limitations, the two of you should be able to work out a way to cover transportation and event attendance. You might, for example, draw up a monthly calendar so you both know how many activities and events require your assistance. Ask your spouse to cover half the tasks, and make yourself responsible for the other half by calling in help and favors if necessary.

The best way to cover kid transport you can't do is to call on other parents. You may at this point have to do some disclosure to people you barely know. Get used to it. You can make up for your absences as a transporting parent by doing such things as taking in kids for afternoons. Giving simple little gifts or sending thank-you cards to people helping you will keep you on good terms. Enlist your kids in helping to find alternative transport. The more open and honest you have been with your children, the easier this whole time will be. Perhaps your school has a kid-carpooling program in place; if not, you can start one. As transportation pool coordinator, maybe you can get off without doing any actual driving.

Reach Out

If there is a school-related problem you don't know how to solve, I recommend you call or write a letter to the school's counselor. That person is trained in therapy, will be familiar with agoraphobia, and could be a good ally. Be open and honest, and ask for ideas and recommendations. You are not the only parent in school with obstacles to overcome, so do not go into this feeling like a freak.

Finally, keep in mind these suggestions for taking care of everyone's needs when it comes to your kids:

> **Balance the books:** The school duties you may have to rely on your partner to perform—including going to school contests, plays, or music performances—can be balanced by such things as taking on all or most of the homework, making lunches, and being the schedule maker.

> **Stop guilt:** It is not appropriate for you to wallow in guilt over the difficulties you may be having in trying to raise kids well while you are quite ill. If someone had hit you with their car and broken your pelvis, you wouldn't be able to take care of any of the usual parent things. Being agoraphobic is neither your fault nor, at the moment, something you can do much about. If you are honest and loving with your children, they will survive this period and be stronger for it. My experience is that people who have had some challenges in their early lives are better prepared for whatever comes at them later than those who have had it easy.

> **Be there:** It's heartbreakingly true that you may not be able to attend all your children's events. Schools often do videos of their events and may be able to provide you with a copy that you

and your kiddos can watch together at home.
If that's not possible, perhaps you can arrange
for someone to video at least the parts involving your kids. Youngsters love to have a good
listener for their stories, so if you pay special
attention—through active listening—to your
children's stories about events, it will be almost
like you were there.

If you are a single agoraphobic parent, the task of
taking care of yourself as well as kid or kids is probably ten times more difficult than it is for a couple.

Friends and Dating

If you are seeking to make friends, or if you are interested in getting romantically involved, read on for a
risk-benefit analysis. Let's talk about romance first. If
you are in a new romantic relationship, or would like
to be, there are some things you need to consider so
you don't create a horrible situation for yourself. We
all know deep down that intimate relationships can
both relieve and create stress. The deliriums of early
romance can make us overlook possible downsides,
however. Be completely honest with yourself while
considering a new love affair.

This venture could have disastrous results, or it
could be very good for you. You are quite vulnerable, alone in your misery, watching others stroll
about with their arms around one another, happy and
carefree. Maybe you could meet just the right person
who could make your cares vanish. Or maybe not.

You already always feel as though you are standing in traffic, so ask yourself this: *Can I afford to make my life even more hazardous by taking up with someone who could either give me a ride or run me over at any time?* Also consider this: you will in a way be *using* that person (more on that in a moment).

Here is an example of how a new romance can be beneficial. I was sixteen, working on a remote ranch in Wyoming, when I was slammed with a recurrence of panic attacks. I was fearful night and day the rest of the summer, but I managed the three-hour drive home with a companion and two cans of beer. When I began my senior year, I got a small part in a school musical as a diversion from my near-constant anxiety. Little did I know, I would sit down and have my makeup put on by the most amazing sixteen-year-old girl on earth, who was just about to make me forget I'd ever even had panic attacks. Her name was Dale. She was cute and hysterically funny, and she flirted with me like crazy. We started dating, and it turned out to be a wonderful teen romance. My panic attacks and anxiety totally vanished on the spot, and they wouldn't return for another two years. I returned to the ranch two more summers.

I know what you're thinking: *It was a kid thing.* True, but I've also experienced a similar phenomenon as an adult. The lesson is that you can at any point in your life become so overjoyed about someone or something or other that your fears go flapping away through an open window. Something of this nature could happen to you, and when it does, be prepared to use the elevated feelings for dual purpose. Take this chance to go on a trip and enjoy the heck out of it if you experience a period of—what shall we call it?— "Spontaneous Diversion."

I once experienced spontaneous recovery without any apparent cause, so I know it can happen. I've read people's comments about this phenomenon in online agoraphobia forums, wherein someone suddenly feels calm after a lengthy period of intense anxiety. I wrote to them advising them to do just as I'm advising you: *take full advantage of magic times.* Remember, sometimes you have to make your own magic. You still have to work out your Recovery Program so you see the big picture, though, so you fully understand *why* you will never have another panic attack.

Full disclosure: I had more negative new romance experiences than positive ones during my years with agoraphobia. In retrospect, I didn't do a good job of presenting the *problem* and didn't have a clue how, or even if, I was going to get over being agoraphobic. You're at an advantage because you know you can get over being agoraphobic and you're working on it. This book helps you pass this knowledge along to others as the need arises.

If you have met someone and the lights went on, proceed with caution. You don't want to hold up your *Warning: Agoraphobia* sign right away because you don't know where this is going. If it keeps going, you will have to reveal your deep dark secret, and you will want to do so in a way the romance can continue to grow without undue stress. Meet in a neutral place for something light to eat so you can talk about some heavy things. Say something like this: "Since you and I seem to both be interested in continuing this relationship, I need to tell you that I suffer from agoraphobia. Do you know what that is? Because even though it's a temporary condition, it could affect our relationship." Introduce the agoraphobia material as well as a summary of your recovery work, and open the floor for discussion. Always remember, it is *your* well-being that is important, so act accordingly. Above all, *do not make foolish promises.* "I don't know" is okay to say.

This period of agoraphobic lockdown is a good time for you to make new friends with whom you'll have a lot in common. Make an effort to connect with like-minded people by starting a peer support group as described in chapter 9. If you are in such a group or another type of therapeutic group, you'll likely stay in touch with some of the people you meet for years. If you're too shy or fearful at this point to begin or go to a group, you can develop friendships with people in the online agoraphobia forums. If you're somewhat mobile, consider doing some volunteer work or joining a book club or other such social discussion group.

You can also become a good friend during this time by getting names and numbers of homebound seniors or disabled folks who would benefit from a weekly phone conversation. A personal visit would be even better—for both of you. The most important thing you can do now is to get connected and stay connected with people who mean something to you.

Bosses

If you are employed and your agoraphobia is affecting your work, it is time to take action before your boss takes action.

Remember, agoraphobia is a condition that resembles a physical illness. If you fell victim to a serious physical illness such as heart trouble or severe rheumatism or a failing kidney, your doctor's word about your condition would probably dictate how your employer would deal with the situation.

For example, if you developed a faulty heart valve and had to alter how and where you worked, your boss could either accommodate you or (heartlessly) fire you. If you were released, you would most likely be eligible for unemployment compensation as well as workers' compensation. Although state laws differ, I think someone forced from work because of agoraphobia should qualify for benefits. If you find yourself in this position, go immediately to your local Job Service office to learn where you stand. You have to be capable of working in order to collect benefits, but there are jobs you could take and jobs you could not take, which should not make you any different than someone, say, with partial paralysis.

The more you can document, the more likely you are to qualify for assistance. I'll say it again: please do not resist applying for help—from all the sources you can find—because if you don't, you will be creating more stress for yourself just down the road. This is the US of A, and we pay taxes to provide for people in a jam. People just like you. If you have been seeing a doctor or therapist, get letters from them to support your claim and print out some poignant information about agoraphobia to include with your application (see chapter 7, "Call in the Pros: Therapeutic and Legal Help").

A lot of people feel like their work defines them, and their relationship to their work becomes as significant as any of their other relationships. Certainly, work is central to most people's lives. We think about work and talk about work and develop friendships through work, and when something traumatic occurs and we can no longer work, what do we do? If only most people could understand how hugely traumatic the loss of work is for an agoraphobic person. Here is one way to explain it to a "normie": "Imagine how frantic you would feel if you loved and depended on your job and suddenly could no longer work. Now imagine someone who (through no fault of her own) became so frantic, she could no longer go to work, so now she will lose her job, which adds frantic onto already frantic. Imagine that. That's me."

I had to leave several jobs over the thirty-year period of my agoraphobia because either I could no longer make the trip to work or being there all day was causing panic attacks. There were also jobs I could have advanced in had I been able to travel. The last job I had to leave because of a recurrence of severe panic attacks was the perfect job for me at the time, and I remember feeling cheated. The setback was so extreme that I applied for and received Social Security disability income; otherwise, I don't know how I would have survived after using up my savings.

If getting to work and being able to stay at work without fleeing has become a problem, you need to arrange a meeting with your supervisor. If you are lucky enough to have an understanding, flexible boss, you may be able to continue working by changing your hours, working fewer hours, or even doing some work from home. This will all depend on educating your employer and significant coworkers about panic attacks and agoraphobia. You can't make significant work changes successfully without your coworkers' support.

If necessary, ask about taking unpaid time off so you can start working on your Recovery Program. In an ideal world, agoraphobia would be just another disability to be accommodated in the workplace. State labor laws differ, but firing someone because of a disability is always a no-no. A layoff is another matter, but you can find out more by calling your local Job Service office.

I think it is true in most states that in order to qualify for unemployment compensation, you have to be capable of and seeking work. If you cannot qualify for unemployment payments, you may qualify for workers' compensation, though state laws differ there as well. If all else fails, your local public assistance office may have a subsistence program you could qualify for until you can receive Social Security disability payments. The sad truth is that a successful, well-educated person could actually become homeless because of agoraphobia.

If your condition has totally disabled you and you have to quit your job, make sure you leave on good terms and have explained the situation to your boss. If you decide to apply for Social Security disability, a supportive letter from your employer will help your claim. Contact your local Job Service as soon as possible and ask about small, part-time jobs you might be able to do. Working at home is much more a possibility now than even ten years ago. If what you find is not enough to support you because of your condition, document that.

You are not going through this for naught. Your ability to inform your employer about mental illness will be helpful to others later on who might face work difficulties because of a particular condition that affects their work.

Teachers

Here are some suggestions to help high school students who are having difficulty because of agoraphobia stay enrolled and succeed, but much of this advice applies to any student. I have some specific remarks for college or post–high school students below.

If you are not able to get to school some days because of high anxiety, and then on days you do get there, you have to occasionally leave class because of panic attacks, go to your school counselor as well as the school nurse. Get them together if you can, because both will be familiar with panic attacks and should be able to help you with a plan that will keep you in school. This is their job, and most of these people love their work. Help them love their work by letting them help you. School counselors and nurses see a lot of kids with anxiety issues. The National Institute of Mental Health reports on its website that a large national survey on adolescent mental health indicates that 13 percent of kids ages nine to eighteen have academic and social problems because of excessive anxiety and that 8 percent of kids ages thirteen to eighteen have anxiety disorders. The most discouraging part of the report is that only 18 percent of these children reporting problems received any mental health care. The counselor will be able to approach teachers for you to help them understand that you may need special considerations for a while. I know it's embarrassing, but maintain your dignity. Look at it this way: you have a unique opportunity to learn about yourself that is going to benefit you. Because of your circumstances, you are learning to deal with your emotions in a way that will essentially make you more mature than your peers.

When you recover, your standing in your community will be uplifted just because of the way you appear, as the new (and restored to former glory) *you*. You'll be different than you were; confident, for example—a virtue that is appealing to nearly everyone (and I mean confident, not arrogant). People see a certain safety in hanging with confident people. So when you recover, get ready to be regarded as an appealing person (not that you weren't already highly regarded) based on the confidence and happiness you exude. True confidence is a state of mind that's hard to hide.

Until that time comes, however, there may be days you cannot make it to school because of your fears.

The plan you develop with the nurse and counselor should include a way for you to get assignments from all your classes to do at home. Schools make accommodations all the time for students with physical illnesses and handicaps. You should get equal treatment. If you are not getting enough cooperation from school, ask a parent to help.

Being inside the typical high school with the chaos of loud, rushing, pushing, crowding teens is enough to give anyone a panic attack. One way to avoid most of that between-class madness is to stay in your classroom writing or reading until just before the next class so the halls will be nearly empty. Another way to reduce your tension during class breaks is to make a friend in each class whom you can walk with to the next class. When I was having high anxiety, I couldn't sit in the middle of a classroom, and I always tried to find a way to be close to the door. If you think this is going to be a problem for you, work something out with your teachers and school counselor. This way, you should be able to get a seat near a door as well as be free to walk out without notice.

While in the classroom, focus on the lecture and your note taking and reading to help you stay cool. Keep a journal-type notebook with you that you can start writing in if you need further distraction from panicky feelings. Get involved with school activities so you have things to do and people to engage with.

If you are in college or other post-high school training or schooling, special accommodations should be easier to obtain. You are an adult now, and most people around you will treat you accordingly. You should be able to schedule most of your classes so you encounter the least amount of difficulty. For example, if your anxiety tends to be higher at a particular time of day, schedule classes around that. High noon was my worst time.

You can take many classes online and even get a degree online, but I hope you won't let your fears force you to avoid the social benefits of higher education. It's beneficial for you to be around people even if doing so is sometimes difficult. When you are in a degree program, you will meet many people with similar interests to your own, which makes communication easier.

The best way for you to heal is to be social around others, because connectedness is *vital* for you. I've been around and can tell you with assurance the following: Almost *everyone* has a vulnerability they're hiding and almost everyone is relieved to learn that someone else (namely you) has some sort of embarrassment and is okay about revealing it. The other person suddenly has a confidant. It's a great way to become friends with someone.

Therapy is more widely available on a college campus than in high school. Your student health center will most likely have a counseling division. If your school offers a counseling degree or has a social work program, you can probably get in to see a graduate student for therapy. Another way to get support is to start a peer support group on campus. See chapter 9 for advice on how to start such a group for people with panic attacks and agoraphobia. I highly recommend you do that, but if you're unable to take on such a task, lobby the student health service to start a specific group. Finally, the best thing about college is you can stop going for a while at any time. Some people take five or six years to graduate, for various reasons. Knowing you can do the work at your own pace should relieve some pressure for you.

Friends and Family

Your close family and your real friends will be with you during all this, but use them wisely. Following are some suggestions to help you maintain this vital support system. It may sound odd, but you might want to think of yourself as the coach of a team of supporters/players. Since you know more about agoraphobia and panic attacks than they do, coach them well so they can be of good use when the coach is having a nervous breakdown and won't come out of the locker room. The arrangement can be as simple as asking, "Is it okay if I call you for a few minutes sometime if I'm having a hard time with anxiety? You're comfortable to talk with."

I recommend that you make out an actual roster to list all the friends and family who will be "playing" for you. Keep close at hand their phone numbers and schedules so you will be able to get in touch with someone in emergencies. Presumably all these people will know you have agoraphobia and know they may be called on once in a while. Make sure you have two or three people on your roster who have agreed to take late-night calls. I got through many a scary night just knowing of a particular person or two I could call. I rarely called anyone at two or three a.m., but knowing I could gave me the cushion I needed to get through the night when panic was threatening.

The best way to get support from those on your roster is to behave as though you are perfectly normal as much of the time as you can. You probably have experience with someone who is always acting needy. Needy people are not easy to be around, while giving people are great to be around. Your relationships will be healthiest if you are perceived to be a giving person who keeps the scoreboard fairly even. Whenever you have to call on friends to help, buy them a little present, do them a favor, send them a card, or at least call to let them know how much you value their friendship and assistance.

You can make shopping trips easier by taking along a friend, or even better, a neighbor or an older family member who no longer drives or doesn't have transportation. Try to make regular connections with your closest allies by just calling to say howdy or to ask what they're doing. Meeting for coffee makes a person feel quite normal (you can sip herbal tea). Social chitchat can be as helpful as therapy sometimes because it gives you a strong sense of connectedness.

9

PEER SUPPORT GROUPS

I benefited greatly from peer support groups over the years, and I have and will continue to urge you to join one or start one. Some of the things I figured out as a result of one particular group led directly to my recovery. Connecting with other agoraphobics face-to-face is like going to a family picnic. You each have so many similarities and familiar stories that you can easily become close allies in problem solving. In fact, the best thing about a support group is the great feeling you get when everyone is working together on the same problem. All for one and one for all.

Organizing a support group will be quite a bit of work, but doing so will benefit you in your recovery as well as be a public service. If you don't want to go it alone, you don't have to. Even if you live in a small town, you will likely find at least one other person with whom you can share organizing duties. This group will become a social forum as well as a therapeutic session, and it will be the job of the facilitator to help focus mostly on recovery plans.

My experience is that if the facilitator does not keep the group mostly focused on recovery, the group will mostly sit around on its fat ass and bitch about the medical establishment. We need to tell our war stories to someone, but try to limit that in a group or it will overtake the proceedings. The best way to get started on the subject of recovery is by introducing a related topic, so having a rotating horror story of the week might be fun and instructive to that end.

Here are some suggestions you can use to start a group as well as a list of things to do once you get started.

Getting the Word Out

There are several ways to spread the word about a peer support group. One time-consuming but safe way is to contact therapists in the Yellow Pages who advertise anxiety work. Mail them letters saying something like: *My name is _____. I suffer from panic disorder and agoraphobia and am interested in forming a peer support group. If you have clients diagnosed with PA and agoraphobia whom you feel might benefit from such a group, please give them my number.* Tell a little about yourself and tell them to call with questions. Therapists are busy people, so persist with follow-ups.

Other ways to publicize include:

- Place an announcement in your local newspapers saying: *A panic disorder and agoraphobia peer support group is being organized here.*

If interested, please call _____. (You could use your phone or get a prepaid cell phone just for this purpose.)

- Do essentially the same as above online, with whatever messaging system would be appropriate. *Craigslist.com* has a place for groups to advertise, for example. You could set up a special email account for the group.

- Post a sign on community bulletin boards with tear-off phone numbers. Print the word *Agoraphobia* in large typeface on your sign so the right people will see it. Mail one to each therapist who works on anxiety and panic to possibly post in their offices.

Organizing

If you don't want to go it alone, now is the time to find someone to help you organize the group. When you talk on the phone, ask people what they have been doing for help and at what level they are—1, 2, or 3 (housebound, partially mobile, mobile with a wall). Also learn when they are available to meet. If it seems like a potentially good fit, you can also ask them how they feel about helping organize a group.

Location

Place is foremost of an agoraphobe's concerns, and despite the limitations, there are ways to meet most needs. Libraries are the ideal meeting place because they are learning centers and support the research aspect of recovery, and they have meeting rooms people can sign up for, as do churches. Some city fire stations have public meeting rooms (in addition to, well, emergency medical technicians and oxygen and other virtues appealing to agoraphobes). If there is a college in your town, you may find a meeting place in a campus building.

Another way is to meet in someone's home. Perhaps there will be two or three people willing to host meetings. One group I was in met several times at the home of a housebound woman. It is somewhat tricky to organize meetings that agoraphobic people can attend (seriously, though, I suppose someone could joke about it). Be flexible and fair in meeting places so the most people get the most benefit. Group members who are more mobile than others could transport those who could only attend if they could ride with someone. Skype and FaceTime are tools that housebound agoraphobes could use to "attend" meetings. If you are organizing this in a large city, you may get so many calls or people will be so far apart that you may have to help organize more than one group.

Preparing Meetings

Meeting once a week will probably be best at first. I strongly recommend you use this book as well as the book *Life Unlocked* by Dr. Srinivasan S. Pillay as your group guidebooks. Dr. Pillay teaches psychiatry at Harvard Medical School and has developed some brilliant insights into panic attacks and agoraphobia. His is the best clinical book I've ever read about folks like us. Well worth the price. *Un-agoraphobic* will help each of you work toward that day when you won't need the group any longer. Ask group members to contribute an idea or two from something they have read or done that was helpful. A research committee could be established to search for and report on developments in agoraphobia treatment.

Order

The role of facilitator can be hard work and should be rotated monthly or so. Most agoraphobic people are orderly, so structuring meetings should come naturally. Each meeting can start with the facilitator introducing herself and talking a bit and then passing the stick around the room. Do whatever it seems most people want, but steer the conversation toward recovery plans if people lose focus.

Topics and Speakers

The facilitator should always ask for a topic at the beginning of each meeting and then do a quick vote to decide whether or not to proceed with the suggestions. I'd suggest shopping as an example of a topic everyone can join in on. You can talk about strategies for store survival, safest stores, best store for open lines, best store for shortest distance to milk, best store for cheery cashiers, and on and on. *Hasn't self-checkout been a blessing? And drive-through pharmacy windows.* An exchange of ideas, strategies, and recovery plans is immensely helpful. Logistics provide good fodder for discussion, like where and how to get your hair cut or coordinating rides for kids. Those and also big-picture topics can be cherry-picked from the pages of this book as needed.

Here is a good way to get guest speakers to come to your group from time to time: call therapists who advertise treatment of anxiety and panic disorder and ask if they would be interested in doing a presentation before your group. The reason this works is there will usually be therapists looking for patients, who would regard it as free advertising.

If starting a face-to-face group won't work, there are other options online. Google, Yahoo!, and Facebook have set up ways for like-minded people to communicate. It is entirely possible to start a subgroup within one social organization or another in order to set up chat groups. You might also look into setting up a phone chat group or a Google hangout (a free group video conference) to help those who sometimes cannot get to a meeting.

A final advisory: the group will function best if you can restrict it to people who have actual agoraphobia resulting from panic disorder. You will have to do the screening on the phone by asking about levels and treatments they've tried and if your symptoms are similar. Questions will arise during group sessions about many aspects of mental illness and the variety of symptoms of anxiety, but your group will progress in a healthy way if you all stay focused on the number-one issue: *overcoming your incapacitating fear of panic attacks*. Don't make it too complicated. I've noted that long-term sufferers of agoraphobia have developed ways to make panic disorder sound medically complex and "psychologically serious" in order to have people grasp its tremendous impact. Analyze your own psychobabble and listen to how others describe their panic disorder. Most of us are too embarrassed to admit that we live incredibly complex lives requiring sophisticated timing and planning, war-like maneuvers, elaborate explanations, and vast reserves of energy because we're afraid of having a panic attack. Keep it simple.

10

HELP FOR ALCOHOLICS

If you are an alcoholic or "problem drinker" because you've been medicating panic attacks, you are probably feeling fairly hopeless at this point in your life.

You used to have only one problem; now you have two. After I heavily self-medicated with alcohol for years, instead of feeling relief, I found myself anxious and depressed all the time, and frankly, I couldn't see a way out. My only medication against the madness of panic attacks was turning against me. I had gone from drinking several quick beers to knock down a panic attack, to drinking every night so I could sleep, to heavy use that was so disgusting and humiliating and endangering, I don't even want to talk about it.

There is good news for you, though. The positive glow that comes from quitting will be of great help in battling any of the old panic that might arise in the first days of not using alcohol as medication.

A Wee Drop for My Nerves

The whole conflagration can begin quite innocently—a snort of brandy to get you across town and through a difficult particular time. Next it's a snifter of brandy to extinguish a panic attack while you're at home. Then you become like the fire department. A little blaze flares up, the alarm goes off, and you pour liquid all over the flaming panic attack, hoping it stays extinguished. These are dangerous times. If you recognize yourself already, I guess you know what you need to do. It won't be easy, but it will be much (insert your own string of dramatic and profane adjectives here) easier to quit drinking now than to quit drinking later. Later could cost you nearly everything you own, including your self-respect and your health.

If you let this alcohol thing get away from you, it will take a tremendous amount of courage and luck and time and money just to get back to the point you are right now. You may be feeling misery at your current level of use, but listen to Uncle Hal: If you don't stop drinking *immediately,* what you're feeling right now will easily compare to paradise in many a recollection of the hell you will go through in chronic alcoholism. If you live to recollect *anything,* that is.

I know exactly how you're feeling about continued use of alcohol. "Please let me keep drinking just enough to get me through the train ride home," or the trip across town for groceries, or just so I can make it to the kids' games, or to help me get through the evening without panic attacks, or the night without waking up (etcetera). That's how afraid we are of panic attacks—we would do almost anything to avoid them, and that's not good because alcohol *can* actually mitigate anxiety for a while. Finally, though, drinking makes everything much worse and that's the unfortunate point at which you cannot stop using it because alcohol is using you.

In truth, alcohol is an agoraphobe's worst enemy the whole time: it disrupts sleep, is a major depressant, and makes anxiety increase because of the hangovers and the sickness that come with long-term use. And then there's the guilt. How can anybody live with being so selfish? By nature, you are the sensitive sort and comprehend it isn't just *your* life that's being affected by your behaviors; anyone who knows and cares about you, family foremost, agonizes over your agony. That doesn't mean you can stop on a dime and quit just because of their concerns. I recall feeling totally trapped. I couldn't stop drinking, so I couldn't overcome panic attacks because I wasn't physically, intellectually, or spiritually capable of doing so, because I couldn't stop drinking.

Look Into Yourself

Now that you know what I *didn't* know—that a person can totally recover from panic attacks—you can start making your plan to quit alcohol as you make your plan for agoraphobia recovery through *Unagoraphobic*. This is not a time to fool around with cutting down or timing your drinking; this is a time to look deeply into yourself in the mirror until you comprehend the basic truth: you cannot recover from agoraphobia without quitting drinking completely and forever. I know the thought of giving up your medication terrifies you. It's all you have, after all, to treat your panic attacks. Guess what, ladies and gentlemen. If you are drinking to excess (and you know who you are), then believe this: at this point, alcohol is *causing* your panic attacks. You might not even be having actual attacks. That was true in my case. I might not have learned that and would have continued pouring down the meds but for the day when I looked up to see three of my out-of-town relatives standing on my front porch.

I maintain there's a difference between the kind of alcoholic who grows up in a bad environment and has lots of the classic markers for becoming alcoholic, and the alcoholic who ends up in a pickle so to speak because of a desperate need to get away from tornado-like panic attacks. But, your title will still be "alcoholic" if you choose the quick, easy way out of a panic attack that alcohol can at first provide. It's not an identity that's easy to carry gracefully.

There's *good news* ahead for you, and you have to believe me because here I am, alive and well to tell about it. So listen up. In addition to daily drinking, I was taking three milligrams per day of Xanax by prescription. I no longer knew the source of my anxiety; I just knew it felt constant. I was sixteen when I first drank specifically to halt panic attacks. Unfortunately, it worked. Had I access to something like this book, I could have found ways to calm myself without drinking. For a long time, my level of drinking mirrored my anxiety levels. I only drank more than a few during periods of high anxiety. When my anxiety lessened, so did my drinking. Unfortunately, the ups and downs over the years eventually led me to become an alcoholic drinker. I could slam down six beers in a very short time when a panic attack had me in its clutches.

Even if you only drink some of the time, long-term use finally creates its own anxiety. Having a panic attack with a bad hangover is one of life's crueler experiences. If you physically have to drink every day, it is time to make a plan to quit. There are many things to consider at this point. If you are, as I was, also taking a benzodiazepine, you are in for a rough stretch of road. I lived through it, and so will you.

Saved by This Book

I advise you to use this book to get your agoraphobia Recovery Program underway so that you can integrate your program to quit drinking. Once you begin to understand how you can take control of your panic and anxiety levels, the thought of losing alcohol as medicine will seem less threatening. Then start a recovery program specifically for alcoholism. Once you start whatever program you discover to quit drinking, put as much energy into that as you do into agoraphobia recovery. The two are closely linked, as you know.

If you are on both benzodiazepines and alcohol, you need to get medical treatment and advice. If your prescriber learns you are drinking with benzos, it's "Goodbye, Mr. Scripts." You've read chapter 5,

"Good Med/Bad Med," so you understand the magnitude of benzo addiction. If you have been taking tranquilizers from this family of medications for more than a month or so, your body is physiologically addicted and you need to work with your doctor on quitting by slowly tapering off. I'm grateful I was able to be in a medical treatment facility when I quit both alcohol and benzos simultaneously. I recommend you only go off both at once if you have some sort of medical supervision. There is something to be said for getting rid of both at once. But it *wasn't* easy.

I shook so badly the first three days in treatment from withdrawal of both tranquilizers and alcohol that feeding myself became problematic. Nothing would stay for the entire ride from my plate to my mouth in even a soupspoon, and forking food seemed comically dangerous as my flailing hand neared my desperate mouth, sharpened prongs endangering my facial features. My new treatment buddy went to the kitchen and brought back one of those two-foot-long stainless steel stirring spoons: problem solved. Luckily, I was giddily happy because I'd actually quit drinking. Endorphins saved me from embarrassment and many other miseries, I'm sure.

A Case for Tranquilizers

If you are medicating only with alcohol (only, ha ha), you may be able to benefit from a tranquilizer if your anxiety gets out of control when you first quit drinking. This could be a hard sell, but even I—former Xanax addict—can see the benefits of, say, two weeks on one of the benzodiazepine family of tranquilizers if early sobriety is accompanied by the kind of panicky feelings you know are the beginning of a bad cycle. If you begin having panic attacks after you stop drinking, show your doctor this chapter and ask about starting a two-week regimen of a benzo, followed with a one-week tapering-off period just to be extra safe. Work extra hard on your Recovery Program during this time. The doctor will probably want to see a month or so of sobriety first. You have a little more suffering to do. Think of it as more material for your memoirs.

Many addiction treatment people I've encountered oppose the use of any chemical "downer" type prescription medications during treatment. I, on the other hand, know that the recurrence of a panic cycle would be devastating for you in a way that no one who has never experienced panic attacks and agoraphobia can comprehend. Period. So I, the former alcoholic and, let's face it—*drug addict*—am saying taking a tranquilizer in the early days of not drinking should be considered if panic attacks resume. However, if you have been taking a benzodiazepine all along, you will have to stop taking that medication before you can recover from agoraphobia (as discussed in chapter 5). In your case, talk to your doctor about short-term use of an SSRI antidepressant; these are being touted as helpful with anxiety.[50]

You may find as I did that after a few days of not drinking, you don't even have anxiety. In that case, you are free to move about the country (as soon as you do your Very Big Trip—see chapter 11). This holistic program I've developed for recovery will help you achieve forever sobriety. I know you're supposed to live a day at a time, but you can also have a new daydream every day.

Extra Help

If maintaining sobriety is going to be a problem for you, consider the least expensive, least constrictive option first, such as regular attendance of Alcoholics Anonymous with a sponsor and the whole program. AA claims it's not a religious organization, but the "higher power" is a significant part of the program, and they pray. So go to a meeting and decide for yourself. If you can work with the program, you're in luck because AA is nearly as ubiquitous as McDonald's.

If AA is not for you, consider starting a peer support group for alcoholics with anxiety disorder. I recommend the Rational Recovery books Jack Trimpey has written.[51] His philosophy of recovery appealed to me because it placed the responsibility on me, where it belonged. That way, I owned the blame for becoming alcoholic and owned the credit for quitting. In AA, the higher power gets the credit for your quitting, but you still have to take the fall for starting in the first place. You don't get to blame a higher power for that, apparently.

If you feel you need additional help, look in the Yellow Pages under "addiction counseling." If you cannot afford individual therapy, most addiction treatment centers offer therapy groups to serve the needs of people whom the law requires to attend. If you feel like you need to go into in-house treatment, you may have to spend a lot of money. Residential treatment is expensive, as it should be. Many states have a sliding-fee addiction treatment center, for which there are usually longish lines. Quitting drinking will save your life. What's that worth? You are about to embark on a wonderful journey to become un-agoraphobic, so don't mess it up. Do whatever you have to do to get off the sauce forever.

What's most important is your *attitude* when treatment or whatever it took to get sober is over and you're on your own. Are you going to be a survivor? Or better yet, a "surthriver" (a combo of *survivor* and *thriver* I just made up to describe the hopeful energy I felt after finishing treatment)? I accomplished a lot in those thirty days in treatment (if doing more self-examination than a narcissist in a hall of mirrors is any sign). I wasn't content to be just a nondrinker. I wanted to accomplish something significant now that I could. Overcoming agoraphobia was, of course, first on my list. So I set about trying to solve the travel mystery. I had been making discouragingly unsuccessful travel attempts on my own for several months when one morning my phone rang and a woman with a low voice said, "Dress for Butte."

11 _____

THE VERY BIG TRIP (VBT)

Here is how to prepare for your Very Big Trip (VBT):
Don't prepare for it.

One of the most sinister forces at work against me while I was trying desperately to be able to travel again was anticipatory anxiety. I would get to a point where I was feeling calm enough to take a little trip somewhere, so I would plan a trip. Each time, I would perseverate about the forthcoming venture and be so worked up when the big day arrived that I would sabotage myself. I would begin the trip at a high anxiety level, which would go higher, and then I would either panic and flee or turn back because I knew the dreaded, familiar panic attack was just around the next corner.

So how are you supposed to accomplish perhaps the single most significant thing you will ever do in your life if every time you plan to do it, you get that old familiar feeling and have to call off the mission? My practical brain was telling me that the better prepared I was for a trip, the easier it would be. Was this correct? Yes and no.

Now I understand that I wasn't preparing in the right way. I was psyching myself up by dwelling on the trip a lot, which served only to keep me on edge. I didn't fully understand the power of intuition or visualizations at the time, or I would have done much more with guided imagery to make the trip less threatening. I would have also laid the groundwork for ways to take spontaneous trips. So, if anticipatory anxiety threatens to get the better of your preparation for the VBT, the visualization exercises in this book can prove useful in your pre-preparation, shall we say.

I'll tell you the amazing, wonderful way it happened to me so that perhaps you can simulate my experience in your life.

I was forty-nine years old and had overcome alcohol and benzodiazepine (Xanax) addiction, and even anxiety for the most part, and had been working for several months on getting over the final hurdle to reach my goal—being able to travel freely. I was living in Helena, Montana, but wanted to move back to my favorite city, Missoula. As noted previously, my attempts at taking trips resulted every time in coming up against a wall I couldn't get through. My panicky feelings would rise in front of me, and I always turned my car around so I wouldn't have a panic attack fifteen or twenty miles from safety (as I understood it). The reaction was reflexive and automatic, seemingly beyond my control. I didn't see how I was ever going to succeed. The harder I tried, the harder it got.

One morning in early March, my close friend and neighbor Kris called and said, "Dress for Butte." I knew exactly what she was up to and quickly put on warm clothes for the trip to the high-altitude mining city sixty miles away. She was in front of my house in two minutes, and I ran out to her car. "Okay, but I'm driving," I said. And we headed for Butte, music playing, a soaring feeling in my heart that I was finally going to succeed in breaking away from the strong gravitational pull of agoraphobia. About twenty miles on our way, I felt like I'd blasted through some sort of barrier. I knew I was free forever. I was too happy to be overcome with heavy emotion. I didn't, for example, get out of the car sobbing and kiss the new ground, but I did smile a lot.

Actually, I'm still smiling. That day, my intuitive friend explained that she knew my fretting over each of my planned outings was the problem, and she solved it for me brilliantly by not giving me any time to fret.

There is a school of therapy for phobias called "desensitization." Exposure therapy is another phrase to describe curing phobia by gradually increasing one's exposure to the feared thing, which in our case is being too far from a safe place. I'm sure this will offend someone, but it's one thing to be an elevator phobic in a closed elevator, which you can exit on the next floor, and another thing entirely to be twenty miles away from safety.

For many years, I tried to force myself to push past my comfort level, but eventually panic attacks always stopped the progress. The result was I got discouraged by the setbacks and gave up trying. Having a panic attack at one time while trying to break free only served to reinforce my fears. My point is, I think you should do the work in this program until you feel calm enough that you could take a little trip. I don't think forcing yourself to travel a little farther each day is a sensible way to recover. Traveling should be fun, or it will never be easy. My advice is to start traveling when you feel comfortable about doing so and to pay attention for spontaneous chances that might come to you out of the blue.

On the other hand, don't let me stop you from climbing into your search engine and looking at exposure therapy, if you like. Apparently it works for some people, and you may find some tricks in that search to help you with full recovery. I just think that forcing yourself might do more harm than good.

Now, let's plan some things you can do so you won't have to "plan" a trip in order to take one. Let's also think of things you can do to make the trip easier. After that, let it go and continue to do positive work until your time arrives. You'll know it. The feeling will be like seeing the first white blossom on an apple tree, hearing the first spring call of a familiar songbird, feeling a cool breeze after a hot day, viewing a rainbow through the mist. The experience will be so fabulous that it'll be corny. Enjoy being corny.

Planning, but Not

Tell the story about my friend Kris and going to Butte to any friends or acquaintances who could possibly play such a role for you someday by sneaking up on you with the opportunity for a trip. Don't suggest anything to them; just tell them the complete story and leave it at that. Toss some seeds to the ground and go on about your business. If one germinates, you may get a pleasant surprise. If it doesn't seem like that way will work, you may have to creatively orchestrate assistance with your trip. To get your way, it's better to have more than one way, remember?

When you feel like you are getting close to being ready for the VBT, try to arrange your life so you could take a spontaneous jaunt on your own if the time felt right. If you make a certain time of each day flex time, you could run errands or go to the library or . . . what else could you do? I know. You could, when the time seemed right, jump into your car and take off on a little trip. This would be a trip you didn't exactly plan, but there's plenty of gas and you have a couple of hours free, so go for it. It may not even be your Big Trip, but a spontaneous trip that takes you beyond your safety boundaries and is enjoyable. That would be excellent preparation for the Biggie.

Your VBT may be much easier if you take it with someone, so start picking out a few someones you could grab to take a quick trip. Have some trip supplies in a satchel convenient to grab for a day trip. This could include music, snacks, binoculars, and anything you know will make the trip as comfortable as possible. If your friend is driving, bring along something for you to focus on if needed for a brief spell of nervousness. You could read aloud from a book of poetry or quotes (or even from this very book you are holding). If you are both good talkers, problem solved.

If you have a particular destination in mind, get a road map of the area so you can break the trip into parts. After my spontaneous trip to Butte, I began planning a solo trip to Missoula, 120 miles away, by studying a map over and over until I knew distances from one landmark or turnoff to another. I found it comforting to know that at a certain point, I'd be a fourth of the way there, and halfway at another point on the map, and so on. You may have several options in mind, which will give you more homework to do. Now that there's Google Earth, you can literally helicopter virtually the whole way and drop down close to see particular things so they will be familiar when you do the actual trip. I'm sure that feature would have been of great help to me at the time, and I hope it will make your journey easier.

If you will be doing your trip solo, have on hand an audiobook or other recordings that will capture your attention if you need a little diversion. Careful listening can be meditative. Humor is an excellent tranquilizer. Here's another electronic suggestion: install a mini video camera on your dashboard and narrate the entire adventure. This would force you to observe and think about your surroundings as you pass through them as well as provide a wonderful record to show the grandkids (and 3.2 million YouTube viewers).

Closely observing my surroundings on my VBT helped me remain centered. I did it not because I understood that connecting with the world around me was a good technique for conquering agoraphobia but because I was traveling through beautiful territory I hadn't seen for thirty years. I was awestruck. Be awestruck on your trip and carefully study everything you see (within the bounds of being a safe driver, of course). I like barns and always think about each one I see, wondering if they smell like the barns I knew as a kid and if there is hay in the loft and a grain room, tack room, etc. If you do something of that nature on your trip, you'll find your surroundings comforting and inviting. Study rural houses and the vehicles around them, and try to guess what the inhabitants are up to. What kinds of crops are being grown on the open land you're passing? If you don't know the names of crops, describe them so you can find out. Advertising signs along the roadways also interest me. I think about the construction and materials and color and lettering styles, and I brainstorm ways I could have made them look and sound better. If there's some interesting geology on your route, study what you'll be seeing in advance so you have something to look forward to. Plus you can make yourself seem extra smart (if only to yourself). "Oh look, an outcropping from the Mesozoic era." Finding things to focus on all the way will strengthen your connection to the world around you and make it all seem safe.

Breathing will be important on the trip and should be naturally easy since you've been doing your daily . . . breathing . . . exer . . . You have been doing your breathing exercises, haven't you?!! That skill alone will make the Very Big Trip a Very Easy Breeze. Wear loose clothing and position your seat belt in the least constrictive way. Get your seat slanted back so that your belly can easily move in and out, blowing new life into you, over and over. Do a bit of easy breathing before you start the trip so you know you can. If a little muscle tense-and-release work will help, this is a good time. If your shoulders start to tighten up on the drive, shrug them up severely so they nearly touch your ears and then force them downward until you feel the muscles pulling across your chest. Another way to keep your shoulders loose is to sit straight up and try to touch your shoulder blades together. (This will bring you very close to the steering wheel. Be safe.) Repetitions of those stretches will help keep you relaxed. We don't want any tight muscles on this journey, so be mindful. *Stay loose* is the word here. If you're not as automatic as you'd like, assure yourself of good deep breaths by posting a couple of notes on the dashboard or console: *Breathe. Be Loose. Have Fun.*

Plan to look as far ahead on the road as you can and imagine yourself being there, picturing the things that will be around you when you get there—what that bunch of trees or pile of rocks will look like when you get close. As you travel on, pick out new sites ahead to study and re-create in your mind. Connection, connection, connection. So important. You will realize that the distant area you're looking at and approaching will be just as comforting as where you are now because you feel very much a part of it just by visualizing your place in it.

As you're driving, think about the confidence you have regained in the struggle to get to this inspiring time in your life. Think about the confidence you have in yourself to deflect any little edgy thoughts you might be having. Flirting with panic is natural at this point, from my experience. Breathe. You may note some familiar scary thinking simply because you've been so overconditioned. I recall feeling a twinge of panic on my Butte trip, but the feeling of exhilaration soon became my only feeling. If you experience a twinge of panic, say hello and goodbye, because it's like a little memory but clearly not the *real thing*. Think about the confidence you have in yourself to take care of anything that comes along. You are the calm, serene, secure center that can provide safety in any storm. If someone needed help and safety and calming, wouldn't you be a good person to come to? You'd be the best.

Smile. The trip you are on is literally the beginning of your amazing new life. Think about this: not many people get to have a new start to their lives. The vast majority is born, does la-de-da and la-de-da, and then dies. Many people in the United States have it pretty easy, aside from some economic problems, a death here, or a divorce there. Those poor innocent people. Do very many of these more normal types ever get to experience the ecstatic, white-hot joy of a life-changing event that is purely, 100 percent positive? My guess is not many people of any kind anywhere get to experience as dramatic a positive change as *you are right now.* You and lottery winners—that's about it. We cannot, of course, forget the price you paid to get to this point of starting a new life. My experience is that getting to wake up every morning with a sense of calm optimism instead

of the old familiar anxiety and dread make those
years of suffering almost worthwhile. It feels so good
when we stop hitting our toe with a hammer.

12

SURVIVAL TIPS

You used to have a certain routine to your life that helped you feel comfortable. Now, needless to say, you don't. The normal times when your life had rhythm and predictability are gone, replaced by chaos. Suddenly there is absolutely no predictability in the day; it's like you are a victim 24/7. Many situations and circumstances that were once a comfortable part of your routine are now fraught with danger. You are completely bewildered. You don't know what the hell to do in this unfamiliar territory.

I've listed several survival tips in the pages to come on how to deal with and get through various frightening situations or circumstances. Some might seem silly, but they worked for me, and I'm sure these tips will at least lead you to invent other survival tactics— things to do or think about at various hard parts of the day to mitigate the terror and overcome a panic attack. Record what works in your journal.

For me, the worst time was night, and I hated going to bed. Let's start there.

Bedtime

I resist routines, but the routine of going to bed at pretty much the same time every night goes along with all the other subconscious training you're doing. If you go to bed every night at eleven, your mind and body will eventually get all systems lined up to get sleepy then. There were several periods in my life when I had to have a bedtime routine, and it worked. I got tired at about that time and felt like going to bed. For me, going to sleep was another thing. Read on.

Meditation techniques are useful for relaxing and going to sleep as soon as you go to bed. If you can't let go enough to meditate at bedtime, make up a little visualization story so you can take a trip to slumber land. If you need a little time before closing the lids, try reading.

Reading in bed worked for me in two ways as long as I had good pillows for it, just the right light with an easy-to-reach switch, and a place to put and fetch my reading material. I could read to make myself sleepy, or I could resume reading if I woke up panicky. It had to be something I could grab quickly, something I could start reading without having to remember a complicated plot, and something that would capture my interest but not stimulate my brain too much. I kept joke books around, essay collections, and spiritual-type books as well as a copy of famous quotations.

Emergency reading material should be soothing and comforting for you. I also kept around at least one book on a subject that I found boring on the theory that I'd get so bored, I'd fall asleep. There are "experts" who say people with insomnia shouldn't read in bed; they should get up and read in a hard chair or on the floor. That may be the way insomniacs want to treat themselves, but we're agoraphobes, trying to make our lives easier, like by staying in the nice, warm bed to read. We're trying to relax, after all. Stay in bed is my expert advice.

Do a toe-to-head muscle-tense-and-release session soon after getting into bed. Start by arching your feet away from you to the count of five and then releasing to the count of five. Arch your feet toward you to the same count; tighten and release as you go up, breathing in as you tighten and breathing out as you release. Tighten and release your calves, thighs, buttocks, abs; shrug your shoulders up, then down; tighten and release your throat and face muscles as you choose them. At that point, go down each arm: your biceps, and then fist clench and release, and finger stretches as you like. Breathe to a regular five-count rhythm throughout. Pause awhile after each release to experience the tingly sensation. Stretch your muscles slowly and cautiously at first to avoid cramps.

. Leg cramps. Now there's something that will take your mind off a panic attack in a hurry.

Learn basic reflexology from a book you can find in a bookstore or a library and give yourself a therapeutic foot massage while you're in bed. Foot massages are actually healing as well as soothing. If you're feeling panicky, pressure on the tips of your toes can give you just enough pain to distract you from the impending doom. Vanquish anxiety with tender loving hands on your feet as well as the feet of others as you get skilled. I'm sure you'll enjoy studying this ancient healing system, which traces correlations between specific places on your foot and places on your body. Doing this regularly will also build strength in your hands.

Sometimes I'd awaken in the middle of the night with a panicky feeling and would have to leap out of bed and get physically active at something to distract me. Luckily, I had clay around in my life, but on top of that, I'd often slam down two or three beers and be able to get back to sleep. Don't do that. Work on one of your projects, particularly the skill you're learning during your workday.

Wear earplugs to eliminate being jarred awake by a late-night car horn or siren. The silicone ones are easiest to put in and take out.

Keep a jar of mentholated salve by your bed. Rubbing some of that inside my nostrils and on my throat and chest helped me get through some scary nights. It reminded me of being comforted for a cold when I was younger. The jolt of it is a good distraction, and if your eyes water, you have to get some tissues to blow your nose. Pretty soon, it will begin to feel like you really are being comforted. It worked for me. Remember . . . *shhhhhh* . . . we're trying to trick our brains into working differently without letting the brain know. *Be sneaky.*

Have a cup of an herbal tea that promotes sleepiness. Chamomile and passionflower are among herbs that have sleep-inducing properties, and there are other concoctions available in health food stores.

Waking Up

If waking up time is stressful for you, here are some suggestions to make your first moments of the day tolerable, leading to enjoyable.

Put your radio or music system on a timer so you can wake up to something that's comforting or soothing—good for your head.

Have a visualization available that you can start doing reflexively as you arise—a guided trip or several you've designed. Take a different head trip each day if you like to get to "serenity space."

Keep your journal beside the bed so you have something to turn to straightaway. If you wake up and start entering data, your mind will soon turn to ideas to add to your Recovery Program. Make a list of things you're going to work on today.

When you stop working on a particular project, leave it in such a way that it's easy to resume. For example, if you're learning a piece of music, put your pencil by the place you want to start; if you're writing something, leave off almost in the middle of a paragraph. That way, if you wake up feeling anxious, you can get out of bed and walk straight over to resume something that was piquing your interest the day before.

Throughout the Day

You already schedule your recovery work activities precisely so you have a specific structure within which to work on your Recovery Program. Stay on task. Stay on task. Stay on task.

Have a poem or short essay or speech around that you are memorizing so you can bring it out to distract yourself long enough to pull yourself out of a nosedive.

Mind your jaw muscles. If your teeth are clenched, it's time to do a whole relaxation routine, top to bottom or the direction of your choice. My jaw was my early warning system, my canary in the mine. Yours might be your shoulder muscles.

Establish a breathing exercise that you can go to quickly in order to calm your system. Work on that every day so if you begin to tighten up and get that desperate feeling, you can bring in the fire extinguisher—a good, deep, satisfying breath. Pushing out your abdomen will cool everything down just like that once you get good at it. Practice quick response.

Avoid the news. You can remain an informed citizen without reading about or viewing stories on horrific human and nature-caused catastrophes, or the unbelievably terrible and stupid things humans do all day every day. Steer yourself toward news of positive things that interest you—mental health, for example. Reading or hearing about catastrophe makes me feel awful and helpless at the same time, not good things for an anxious person to feel. Send money, even two dollars, to the relief organization instead of reading about the horror. Feel good that you helped.

Have a code word—*unlax!*—or something like that to trigger a relaxation response. Pretend you're one of those stage hypnotists who does a posthypnotic thing to put someone under. "When I count to three, you are going to become verrrrrry relaaaaaxed. One . . . twooooo . . . "

Say hello to strangers in your proximity throughout the day. Some people won't respond to your not-so-common-anymore courtesy, meaning they are in need of a little connection to the world. I venture that most everyone you say hello to will remember it later on in the day as a nice little experience. (Little do they know, you were doing it for purely selfish reasons. Hee hee.)

Get the biggest, industrial-strength vibrating massager they make and keep it handy as needed through the day. The rumble and the shake will loosen your tight muscles as well as your tight mind.

The Social Scene

You probably avoid social gatherings when your anxiety level is fairly high for fear your tension will escalate to a panic attack. Either that or you drink in order to socially engage, in which case, see chapter 10, "Help for Alcoholics," posthaste. Following are some tips to help you have a good time in social settings.

Here is a suggestion for the dreaded task of entering a room of unfamiliar faces. Look into the distance, smile, and wave your hand slightly as though you've just seen someone and that will give you a "reason" to move purposefully toward the food. Do not linger at the door where everyone can look at you. People who hang around the food are easier to talk to than other strangers at a gathering. If they're there longer than to pick up a radish and a couple slices of cheese, they're there for a reason, probably the same reason as you.

As soon as you spot that certain someone—that person who appears at least as uncomfortable as you—enlist her as your ally. First, say this: "I'm afraid to try that (point) dip because it looks like it has fish. What do you think? I don't really like fish." This will initiate some activity and more chitchat, at which point you can reveal your anxiety about crowds, which will serve to relieve your anxiety.

I discovered early in my journalism career that interviews are actually a snap because most people love to talk about themselves and their achievements (though not so much if they are *under indictment* for their achievements). All you have to do is ask a few good questions. For example, if you're at a social function with people you've not met and you get introduced to someone, ask what the person does and then follow it up with, "Can you tell me more about being a (welder or baker or . . .)? I've always been curious about it. How did you get started?" Tactics such as this will not only get you off the hook but will also make you the kind of person people like to hang out with. You, of course, can use this approach to getting comfortable with people anywhere; it doesn't have to be a group.

Each time you interact with someone face-to-face or on the phone, imagine you are that other person. Imagine that person is having personal difficulties that you could actually help resolve just by demonstrating gentle respect.

Diversions—Enduring and Thwarting an Attack

One way to deflect an incoming attack is to start chanting. I began using a classic Buddhist chant to help settle my jangled nerves. There are many Tibetan monk chants, but the Lotus Sutra is what worked for me. I was told it means something about studying the perfection of the lotus blossom with a Buddha nature to see mystic universal law or understand the Universe. The notion of focusing on the organic beauty of nature and the sound I made with the chant helped me fend off some bad spirits. Phonetically, the chant is broken up thusly:

> *Nam myo ho ren ge kyo,* but it's usually seen written as: *Nam-my oho-renge-kyo.*

I listened to monks chanting the phrase without pauses, which made it easier. Establish a rhythm that feels good to you, and then repeat it for a couple of minutes. I (sometimes) chant while I'm in difficult traffic. To anyone looking your way, it just looks like you're singing. Use chanting also to help you get to sleep at night.

Repeating a song or some calming saying that you can start into quickly will help you avert a panic attack if you can instantly focus on the diversion. That's what you'll be training yourself to do. Be safe: have a well-worn chant, a distracting song, and a comforting saying on hand so during that time when clear thinking is a challenge, you could chant, you could sing, or you could recite. My favorite was "Oh What a Beautiful Mornin'" from the musical *Oklahoma!*

Exercise can be great, but if you're facing down a panic attack, don't run. You may find it easier to take on the attack if you're doing some sort of movement, though. You do have a lot of energy to release. Do some rhythmic walking so you're taking, like, three long steps with a shorter step and then two and then five, so you have something to focus on and gain the release benefit of at least some movement, with *counting.* Counting can be a calming activity.

If you think you'll rely on counting in an emergency, decide on this in advance so you can automatically go to counting blue cars or azalea bushes—anything that requires you to be searching objectively through your immediate environment. Connection to your surroundings will save you.

A camera is a good tool for focusing on things other than your anxiety. Take one along so if you begin to have trouble with too much stimulus, you can pause and look at a specific area through the lens; fixate on what you see there, and then pan on to another scene; fixate on that as well, and continue until you've calmed down—and gotten some memorable photos. Put them in your journal with notes.

Electronics will help distract you through some hard times, but you should focus on graduating to diversions you can do with your mind alone. Reasons: you can't operate a vehicle safely and concentrate on screens. No no no. Diversions you create will work best because they're designed just for you.

Begin following an organization you believe in and supporting it by reading about what it's doing and contributing in some way. Getting involved with an organization or movement that you feel passionately about gives you a strong connected feeling as well as a warm heart for helping out.

Reaching out in whatever way you are able will benefit doubly. Folks who heat with wood say it warms them twice, once when they cut and chop it and once when they burn it. See what I'm getting at? Your activities for a cause will warm twice.

13

THE BENEFITS
OF AGORAPHOBIA

Who knew? Here we are, dwelling on all the negative, awful liabilities inherent to agoraphobia when there are so many positive things about your condition that can be of benefit to you and society. I'm just trying to point out that agoraphobia is not all gloom and doom. Maybe a few will make you smile, if I'm lucky. And a smile won't kill you. Let's look at some of them.

Energy Conservation

According to the US Department of Transportation website, the average American drives fourteen thousand miles a year, and there are an estimated 190 million licensed drivers in this country. Nearly 2 million adults in the United States have agoraphobia and probably aren't doing much driving at all.[52] Let's say about half of those drive at most twenty-five miles per week, which is thirteen hundred miles per year, or 12,700 fewer miles per year than the "normies." The average car gets twenty-three miles to a gallon of fuel, according to the DOT, meaning the average driver uses 552 gallons of gas a year while the agoraphobic driver uses about fifty-seven gallons. This means you personally save your country nearly five hundred gallons of fossil fuel a year because of your agoraphobia. Add in your contribution to cleaner air and you, my friend, qualify as an American Hero.

Saving Resources

Imagine how long your vehicle will remain mechanically viable with you driving only about thirteen hundred miles per year. The average car, according to a DOT estimate, lasts 150,000 miles, which means your car will provide eighty-six years of continuous service! Nothing to sneeze at. Of course, your particular car might not be brand new and, if you use this book, you will start driving more at some point, so the figures could change. You can do the math on that at your leisure.

You Are a Job Creator

Imagine how many additional people have been put to work at various online stores and delivery businesses because you can't go shopping in person. I'm a little fuzzy on that kind of math, but when a couple of million people with agoraphobia want everything delivered, that's got to add up. Plus, it's not like actual stores have to lay people off just because you seldom come in anymore. In fact, if you are like most agoraphobes, you have left behind approximately six half-full grocery carts over the past three years when you fled the premises in panic. That has meant extra work for the stockers who put your groceries back on the shelves. At half an hour's work per cart, you have given stockers of America at, say $9.15 an hour plus benefits, an extra thirty bucks over the last three years. That may not sound like much, but multiply it by 2 or 3 million people like you and it becomes clear that agoraphobes contribute significantly to the economy. Also, think how many therapists would be out of work if not for our kind.

Shorter Lines

Waiting in line is one of life's more vexing activities. Because agoraphobic people do not for the most part stand in line, lines everywhere are that much shorter. But do we get thanks? This is yet another of the ways agoraphobes benefit society without being properly credited.

New Careers

There are professional acting schools in most major cities, theater departments at most colleges and universities, community theater groups all over the place, touring theater and production companies, but nowhere is there a better place to train for work as a thespian than the Agoraphobia Acting Academy.

Think back on the award-winning performances you've given over the years explaining away this or getting out of that. You have been writer, producer, director, and actor in many a brilliant improvisational whopper as one threat or another appeared before you. You will be very convincing in any role you play on stage, in the movies, or on television. Don't forget to send us your autographed publicity photo.

Or would you rather be a cruise ship director? All the manic energy and elaborate planning you employ every day in order to organize and control your life could, instead, organize and control five hundred people on a boat going to Fiji. You? Going to Fiji? Yikes!

Giving Hope to Others

There are tribes of doorknockers out there, mostly people who really really want you to be the way they are so they won't feel so insecure about being the way they are. A homebound agoraphobe teetering on a panic attack will quickly open the door to anyone who doesn't look like an ax murderer just to have a diversion—someone, anyone, to talk to and talk to and talk to. This gives hope if only briefly to a proselytizer and gives you, the desperate, quivering mass of fear and anxiety, relief for now from a doozy of a dance with your devil. Your need meets their need, and what more could we all hope for from life? You made their day—at least until they figured out your game. You were probably the only person to ever witness a "Witness" looking repeatedly at her watch and saying, "I'm afraid I really must be going."

Free "Exercise"

One thing most agoraphobes do not do well is exercise in traditional ways. You may have been feeling needlessly guilty because you have not joined the rest of the world in the oxygen-depleting activities the normies seem to feel the need to perform. They are everywhere, aren't they? You see them running through streets and parks, riding their bikes, swimming laps, hitting and throwing and running after balls of one kind or another in order to raise their heart rates enough to constitute exercise. What fools they be. A fully developed agoraphobe can go to a crowded movie theater and, just by sitting toward the front, ten seats in from the aisle, get the same elevated heart rate benefit your average jogger takes several hours and the risk of being run over to attain. Plus you get to watch a movie you will never forget. I, for example, will never forget *Out of Africa*. I thought neither I nor Meryl Streep would *ever* get out, but when I finally did, I was very fit.

And don't overlook isometrics, the exercise system that pits muscle against muscle made famous on TV but actually invented hundreds of years earlier by agoraphobes whose muscles are always tensing and releasing, tensing and releasing—because we're nuts.

Take a Little, Give a Little

Which do you want first? The good economic news you're responsible for? Or the bad economic news you're responsible for? Oh heck, I'm writing the book; I'll pick. The *bad news* is, you cost a lot of people a lot of money. The National Institute of Mental Health estimates $42 billion a year is lost to the US economy because of anxiety disorders. Now, see, we have the bad news out of the way and get to enjoy dessert with the good news. Here it is: You, Mr. and Ms. Big Pockets, are rewarding the Pharmaceutical Industrial Complex to the tune of $18.2 billion a year just in antianxiety medication. Oh wait, that's only good news for them. I guess it's *all* bad news for you—for now. Sorry.

There are many more ways you are good and important, but you get the point, I hope.

14

LETTER TO THE PARTNER

If you are married to or in a serious relationship with someone who either recently became or has now revealed they are agoraphobic, you will probably have to make some drastic adjustments if you want the relationship to survive. There is always more than one victim when mental illness is in the picture. The first thing you both need to do is learn as much as you can online or in articles and books about panic disorder leading to agoraphobia so you can have an informed discussion. You'll learn a lot from this book. The easy news is, your partner can totally recover from agoraphobia; the hard news is, it could take awhile.

You may find it difficult to comprehend how panic attacks can totally take control of a person's life, but this is what happens with agoraphobia. Panic attacks are terrifying beyond description and can make it impossible for the person you love to do some of the things you used to enjoy doing together. Your loved one cannot "snap out of it" or be better by next week.

Agoraphobia is difficult business because the triggers lie in the subconscious, and your partner at this point has very little if any conscious control over what is happening and is terrified 24/7 by the prospect of having another panic attack, which in turn is what all the anxiety is about.

Think of your automatic startle reflex and magnify it. When, say, someone jumps out in front of you from behind a corner, you make a loud sound and quickly move or freeze. Your heart rapidly speeds up. You were scared to death there for a second. It would be difficult, and seemingly foolhardy, to change your central nervous system so *nothing* that happened around you could startle you. This is more or less the sort of change your partner is working on. The reflex that triggers an adrenaline flood originates in the most primitive part of the brain and was for a long period of humanoid history absolutely essential for survival. The projects and activities and information in this book help your partner learn new ways of operating the operating system. By doing this, something innocuous that would merely startle you will no longer have the power to send your loved one into a full-blown panic attack.

Remember, your brief experience with high anxiety is that it disappears as soon as you understand you are not in danger. The agoraphobe's system, unfortunately, is exceedingly difficult to stop once it gets going. The startle reflex turns into a seven-alarm fire, and your partner is unwittingly throwing gasoline (adrenaline) onto it because that's what the cave dweller manual says to do. The greater the adrenaline flow, the higher a person could climb or run or whatever was needed to get away from a people eater.

All the old ways of responding to "danger" in the subconscious part of the brain have to be changed. Making these changes will take time, but how much is difficult to predict. If you can think of your partner as having been in a terrible accident that will require you to be nurse and near-constant companion for an unknown amount of time, you won't be far off.

You need to be honest with yourself, because your emotional survival is part of the big picture. If you know you cannot survive living with an agoraphobic person, start preparing for a separation in such a way that will minimize the trauma. A divorce or separation will be very hard on your partner but better in the long run than a dishonest relationship with both of you feeling angry and resentful. Do not, please, feel guilty if you have to separate.

If you decide to stay together, I recommend couples counseling of some sort so you will have an idea of what to look for and prepare for. The following are things you need to be absolutely certain you are okay with in order to maintain a close relationship with an agoraphobic person:

1. You cannot have expectations. The person with agoraphobia has no clue at this point when or even if he will recover from this bizarre and crippling condition. Setting time limits would be cruel and counterproductive.

2. Unpredictability is part of the phenomenon. Your partner may have periods of time of being able to get out and accomplish things, only to be followed by periods of hyperanxiety and immobility. Mood swings from excited happiness to dark depression are common and may seem baffling but are usually related to particular stressors.

3. You won't do vacation traveling as a couple. You cannot not travel just because your partner has this affliction, but both of you will for now miss out on the relationship-enhancing joy of vacationing together. The two of you won't be "getting away from it all." You need to be able to travel as much as your relationship allows. Include your partner in helping plan your vacations so that will come naturally when you are able to travel together. You two may want to try small trips, but don't be surprised if you often have to turn around and come back after an attempted outing, particularly in the early going of recovery. The travel issue could be a difficult bridge for you to cross, but please read chapter 11 about taking trips to learn how you could play a role in the climax of this story, taking on the mantle of Kris.

4. Movies and indoor concerts are probably out, depending on your partner's level at any particular time. Wherever people go that involves crowds and waiting in line, you will probably be attending alone. If you have children, you might be taking them to all the indoor activities such as sports

contests, recitals, and plays. You also may have to be the parent-conference parent. Please believe me: the agoraphobic person would give anything to be able to engage in all these activities, but going out and getting caught up in swarming activities is more difficult than you can ever know for someone with panic disorder.

5. Sex and romance may disappear from time to time as your partner's anxiety level rises and falls. You might think sex would be a great diversion and you could actually cure someone in the bedroom but, sorry, that probably isn't going to happen. When agoraphobic people are in or near a panic state, they do not want to be experimenting with their emotions. A massage, on the other hand, can help reduce anxiety, and massages can be fun.

6. Anaïs Nin, French and American writer and famous lover, said this: "Anxiety is love's greatest killer. It creates the failures. It makes others feel *as you might* when a drowning man holds on to you. You want to save him, but you know he will strangle you with his panic."[53]

The good news is, your willingness to stay with the madness of agoraphobia may pay big dividends when your partner recovers. I know recovery will happen if she works hard at it, but you don't know that. Therefore your decision to stay together will be a leap of faith, and how often does one get to experience that? I can tell you that when your partner recovers, celebration will be in the air for a long time and you may find yourself in a whirlwind of catch-up activities. The change will be so dramatic, in fact, that the two of you should talk about the possible ramifications, which may even involve moving. The recovery could be a long time from now, but you should be prepared to live with a good-as-new, ecstatically happy person.

15

GRADUATION SPEECH

This is for you to read after you've taken your Very Big Trip and know that you are free and ready to start your new life. This is the speech that all graduates of *Un-agoraphobic* get to hear, summing up results of what might be the most amazing thing you've ever done. It's from me, the book you're holding—hi! You conquered, and now you rule. At one time, you didn't think it possible to be where you are now, at the back of this book where anything—heck, *everything*—is possible.

You've heard of talking books. Well, let me tell you that this talking book feels both sad and happy when we arrive at the end of me, my last few pages. I'm really happy for you, that you are in such a beautiful place, but I'm . . . a little, um . . . not really sad, more like *nostalgic*. It is kind of our last time together before you, *sniff,* leave the nest, and we don't get to hang out so much anymore. I hope you'll drop in and browse a little from time to time, at least pick me up, say hello, blow the dust off, until it's time to pass me along. I know you'll make new friends far from here and you'll be busy, so . . . I wish you well . . . and don't worry about, *sob,* me.

Before you go, though, I have a few parting thoughts:

(Just a second . . . I see some newbies peeking in here.) "Sorry folks, you in the back there, if you're not a graduate, ready to take the next exit, this part of the book will be here for you when you are ready to graduate. You don't want to get ahead of yourselves. It's the other end of the book you want. Chapter 15, "The Graduation Speech," is supposed to be a special time at the end of the book for, well, me and the graduates. You understand. So if you could just . . . go back to the front . . . ? And start there, at the beginning? Thanks. Hope to see you soon . . . "

Okay, somebody close the doors. We'll just wait a little bit for them to return to the first chapter . . . and . . . are they gone? Okay. I gotta ask you just one thing:

How does it *feel* to be *free?!!!* You probably have so many feelings, you can't count them. I bet gratitude is one of the strongest of your feelings, though. By the way, did I tell you this was costing you five hundred bucks? Just kidding. Aside from the cost of buying me, it's free to be free (of course we're not at this time counting the doctors, hospitals, therapists, lost this and lost that). And I, the book, wouldn't be experiencing freedom if it weren't for you, by the way. Thanks a million. You don't know how humiliating it is to be sent back to the cold, dark warehouse.

Oh sure, I'll be lonely and I'll miss you, but I'll survive, so long as I don't have to *remain* on a shelf. I prefer to keep busy, so when you're sure you don't need me any longer, perhaps you know someone who could adopt me and run their fingers through my pages until they're cured, and then pass me along to another future traveler to win her victory, and so on. Each of those readers will, of course, want to buy their own copy when they pass along yours.

And it came to pass that you did give me to someone else who gave me to someone else and on and on, and I became so well traveled throughout the land after I left you that I no longer knew my way home—to you. Here's my story about that sometimes-lonely period with the amazingly serendipitous conclusion:

After your friends all finished with me (some of them, your father included, hardly even glanced at me, I feel I must report), I ended up on a cross-country trip in a VW bus being driven by a woman who had read me ferociously for several months. And then one day, I and all my house companions got compressed into her little box of a vehicle. It was exciting to know she was making her big trip because of me, but I didn't hear or see any of it, buried as I was in a milk crate beneath five hundred pounds of clothing and Emily Dickinson. Em was an exquisite traveling companion and, I must say, not as shy as she's been made out to be. Did you know she was agoraphobic? Yes . . . and I helped her make the trip. Just think. Little old me helped Emily Dickinson.

Anyhoo . . . my last day in the United States was when some nutty bookworm bought me at Aunt Bonnie's Books in Helena, Montana, and then took me to the No Sweat Café, where he placed a call to Paris and began speaking excitedly in French to someone named Simone. The next day, I was wrapped in paper and put on a flight to the City of Lights, where Simone and several people in her group she started as a result of chapter 10 traded me back and forth. Eventually, I was put into a box with lots of other books and spent a long time waiting, which is what books do. We wait to enlighten. We'd rather be busy, though.

I recall being awakened, moved into a car, and driven to a back alley second-hand bookstore on the Left Bank. A few months later, the shop closed and the entire inventory, including me, was sold to a bookstore owner in the provinces. I landed on a low shelf covered by a heavy volume of quiche recipes and assumed that would be my final resting place. "'Un-agoraphobic' Latest Self-Help to Fall Victim to French Cookbooks" would have probably been the title of my obituary in the *New York Times* book reviews section. It could have been worse. At least it *sounds* romantic.

And then one sunny June afternoon, you'll be having lunch on the front porch of your small villa in southern France when a person of the attractive sex you've never seen before opens your garden gate and proceeds serenely up the stone path toward you with a small brown paper bag in hand.

"Monsieur/Madam/Mademoiselle, (your name here)?"

You nod warily.

"I found your name"—only it's all in French, which you can understand and speak because you studied it during your recovery work with *Un-agoraphobic*, after which your renewed ability to travel allowed you to become financially well off, which is why you're living in southern France—"written in the front of this book. I live in the village. Bernard (bookstore owner you've become pals with) told me you live here."

The person then reaches into the bag and pulls out a familiar-looking volume whose cover is torn and patched and the back is stained with something dark . . . and many pages are dog-eared and droopy, but when the person opens the cover and points to where you wrote your name on me, I almost cried. So did you, admit it. *Together again!* after all these years. Just like *Old Yeller*. The mysterious stranger cradles the book in both hands and then brings it to her/his heart saying, "Free at last, thanks in part to you," and hands it to you, the person who originally bought the book, making it possible for this person to stoop over in a bookstore to pick up a book of quiche recipes, when lo and behold, a word appeared, *agoraphobic*, which this person understood all too well.

"Merci," this person says and then turns and walks back up the path.

You now get to finish the story your way. You obviously have been financially successful; even these *mini* villas are up in . . . well, several figures, but are you successful in relationships as well?

As this is going down, is your perfect partner inside paring pears, or have you become unpaired and therefore prepared to pursue this person up the primrose path? You would certainly have a lot to talk about. But that's *your* life. Stay tuned. As for me, I hope you'll now finally return me to the bookshelf just as I am—battered and torn, blood- and tear-stained, in short, put to good use.

You know where I'd be happiest in retirement? Either in with whatever spirituality and philosophy volumes you have or with the poetry books. Better yet, between the two, getting my just revenge by living a good life. Just think, yours truly in with two of the greatest ever members of the book community: philosophy and poetry. I don't suppose you have any Emily Dickinson?

But Enough about Me . . . the Book

I, the writer, hope you will keep your journal going through this period. The newfound freedom was a surreal time for me. I had lived with a ball and chain for a long time, and all of a sudden . . . it was gone. I felt entirely free and confident, even though I was a man without a plan. I moved back to the city I'd left seventeen years earlier, but I had no idea how I'd make a living. Being so untethered would have freaked me out the previous years, but now being untethered gave me tremendous happiness and confidence. I hope you find similar circumstances. If you'd like to write about your experience, there's a "Free At Last!" section in the *Un-agoraphobic* newsletter (*www.unagoraphobic.com*) for brief stories by folks who have recovered or have had dramatic successes.

I don't think my feet touched the ground as I walked the mile or so back to my new apartment after dropping off the U-Haul truck I'd rented to move to my new city and begin my new life after thirty years in agoraphobia prison.

It was mid-May, sunny, and a perfect spring day in Missoula, Montana, the place to which I'd dreamed so long of returning. My new free-from-agoraphobia world was a laughing baby, a bluebird on my shoulder, an all-day rainbow, a basket of puppies. It was unbelievable. My smile muscles ached. This went on and on. Every morning, you will wake up in a good mood. Every morning. Until you get used to it, that is. Then you'll be grumpy once in a while, but that's perfectly okay.

Everything seemed to work and fall into place and be there when I needed it as I began my new life. I got an unbelievably great apartment right off the bat and soon had a couple of part-time jobs. Looking back, I think my chronic optimism helped pave the way. I know how well I respond to bright and shiny people, and I'm sure I qualified as one of those for at least several months after my recovery. Unfortunately, you won't stay high forever—happy forever, but probably not high forever. Enjoy every day of your new life, graduates. There is a lesson to be learned, though, about how we present to others. When we present as optimistic and honestly confident, we allow others to trust us and feel comfortable around us. In other words, to succeed in your new life, just be your (new) self.

In summary, graduates, I warned you that recovery would be hard work, and I'm sure you'll now agree. Your hard work and creative solutions got you where you wanted to be, however, and those same two attributes will help you enjoy a unique, useful, richly rewarding life.

And in Conclusion . . .

Following are some ways to maintain your new way of being.

1. Keep your journal going through this period. I wish I'd recorded my thoughts just to see how delirious my writing would have been. Take lots of photos and write daily for at least the first two months. I'm serious, my friends—this will be always your proudest moment (or close), so honor it by recording it. There's an even more important reason for maintaining a journal: you are no longer a junk heap; you are now a high-performing, stunning Ferrari and should have regular maintenance and tune-ups. You can maintain your high standards by checking in with your journal mechanic regularly, say once a week.

2. If you didn't start a peer support group as I recommended (*tsk tsk*), this would be a good time to do your community a favor by organizing one. A group I helped start helped me recover because a woman who had recovered by using some kind of program began attending just to help out. She was generous with her knowledge, slim as it was in those days before the Internet, and acted as a cheerleader. It wasn't really anything specific she said—just some general sorts of things people could interpret for themselves. Having her example was what was helpful to me. She seemed so serene and happy all the time because she had recovered. I desperately wanted to follow her example, and I did, and that is why I'm asking you to pass it along by starting a group.

3. If you start to get in trouble again, overwhelmed by something that threatens to return you to panicky feelings, it's the *breathing* that will get you out of trouble every time. Whenever you're in any kind of anxiety-provoking situation, stop and focus on your breathing. Your meditation practice makes it possible for you to focus on a single task, that of arranging your body and mind so it is possible to take deep, healing, calming breaths whenever you want. I mention this because the first time I had panicky feelings after my recovery was quite disturbing. The experience made me fear I was slip-ping back into it, but luckily I instinctively started loosening my muscles and breathing in deeply and slowly. You are over this, but you may still get some of those old scary feelings once in a while. Relax. Breathing works every time.

4. Pass it on.

NOTES

1. *The Brain Book* by Ken Ashwell, Firefly Books 2012, pp. 34–35.

2. Ibid, p. 283.

3. "Extreme Fear" by Jeff Wise, *Psychology Today*, Nov. 4, 2010.

4. *Train Your Mind, Change Your Brain* by Sharon Begley, Ballantine Books 2008, pp. 7–10.

5. *The Brain Book*, pp. 34–35.

6. *The Psychology of Humor* by Rod A. Martin, Elsevier Academic Press 2007, as cited on the website for the Association for Applied and Therapeutic Humor, *www.aath.org*.

7. Indiana Jones was a professor/explorer character in several adventure movies starting with *Raiders of the Lost Ark* in 1981. The character used a bullwhip for several purposes and often ended up in dark, scary, mysterious places.

8. *The Brain Book*, pp. 55–56.

9. "Unleashing Creativity" by Ulrich Kraft in *Best of the Brain from Scientific American* ed. by Floyd E. Bloom, Dana Press 2007, p. 9.

10. Drawing on the Right Side of the Brain series by Betty Edwards, Penguin Group 1979.

11. *The Neuro Revolution* by Zack Lynch, St. Martin's Press 2009, pp. 124–25.

12. "The Mind Made Visible," by Semir Zekli in *Mapping the Mind* by Rita Carter, University of California Press 2010, pp. 19–22.

13. *The Elements of Style* by William Strunk Jr. and E. B. White, Pearson Education, Limited, 2013.

14. *The Buddhist Handbook* by John Snelling, Inner Traditions 1991, pp. 18–23.

15. Ibid, pp. 116–120.

16. Ibid, p. 56.

17. *Train Your Mind, Change Your Brain*, pp. 222–226.

18. Ibid, Preface.

19. My definition of *humanist* is "one who focuses on the achievements of humans through self-determination as opposed to divine influence."

20. *The Buddhist Handbook*, p. 46.

21. Ibid, pp. 43–45.

22. *Black Elk Speaks* by Black Elk and John G. Neihardt, University of Nebraska Press 1989.

23. *Thoreau: A Book of Quotations* by Henry David Thoreau, Courier Dover Publications 2012.

24. *Train Your Mind, Change Your Brain*, pp. 36–37.

25. Anxiety and Depression Association of America, *www.adaa.org*.

26. Ibid.

27. "Barbiturate History" by Ananya Mandel, *NewsMedical*, *www.news-medical.net*.

28. *The Age of Anxiety* by Andrea Ton, Basic Books 2009.

29. Ibid.

30. "The Role of Serendipity in Drug Discovery" by Thomas A. Ban, *Dialogues in Clinical Neuroscience* Sept. 2006.

31. Ibid.

32. *The Essential Guide to Psychiatric Drugs* by Jack M. Gorman, St. Martin's Press 2007, and personal interviews with mental health prescribers.

33. Ibid.

34. Ibid.

35. Ibid.

36. Ibid.

37. Ibid.

38. Ibid.

39. *The Brain Book*, p. 253.

40. "Health Benefits of Lemon," *Organic Facts, www. organicfacts.net.* Lemon juice can treat throat infections, indigestion, constipation, strokes, and kidney stones, among other conditions.

41. "Chemical Cuisine," *Center for Science in the Public Interest, www.cspinet.org.* The website lists most food additives, categorizing them as "safe," "caution," and "those to avoid."

42. "9 Amazing Health Benefits of Berries" by Madeline Vann, *Everyday Health, www.everydayhealth.com.*

43. *Optimum Nutrition for the Mind* by Patrick Holford, Basic Health Publications Inc. 2004, p. 6.

44. Ibid, p. 49.

45. Ibid.

46. Ibid.

47. *The Diagnostic and Statistical Manual of Mental Disorders*, 5th ed., American Psychiatric Association 2013.

48. *The Adventures of Tom Sawyer* by Mark Twain, New-South Books 2009.

49. "Cost Outfitting Soldiers Spiral Up" by Pauline Jelinek, *USA Today* Oct. 2007.

50. *The Essential Guide to Psychiatric Drugs*, pp. 154–155.

51. Jack Trimpey wrote two books in the Rational Recovery series: *The Small Book* (as opposed to the AA *Big Book*), Random House 1995, and *Rational Recovery: The New Cure for Substance Addiction*, Simon & Schuster 1996.

52. "The Numbers Count: Mental Disorders in America," *National Institute of Mental Health*, *www.nimh.nih.gov*. The website statistics estimate that nearly 1 percent (.8 percent) of people in the US population of 317 million (based on 2012 census) suffer from agoraphobia.

53. *The Oxford Dictionary of Quotations* ed. by Elizabeth M. Knowles, Oxford University Press 1999.

ABOUT THE AUTHOR

HAL MATHEW was born and raised in Billings, MT. He began his writing and editing career at The Billings Gazette. Despite being plagued by panic disorder and agoraphobia, his journalism career included several other newspapers and a wire service. With Un-Agoraphobic he has created a way for those suffering with continual anxiety and panic attacks to reclaim their lives. He makes pottery, gardens, and writes in his adopted home of Salem, Oregon. Visit Hal online at www.unagoraphobic.com.

TO OUR READERS

Conari Press, an imprint of Red Wheel/Weiser, publishes books on topics ranging from spirituality, personal growth, and relationships to women's issues, parenting, and social issues. Our mission is to publish quality books that will make a difference in people's lives—how we feel about ourselves and how we relate to one another. We value integrity, compassion, and receptivity, both in the books we publish and in the way we do business.

Our readers are our most important resource, and we appreciate your input, suggestions, and ideas about what you would like to see published.

Visit our website at *www.redwheelweiser.com* to learn about our upcoming books and free downloads, and be sure to go to *www.redwheelweiser.com/newsletter* to sign up for newsletters and exclusive offers.

You can also contact us at *info@rwwbooks.com*.

Conari Press
an imprint of Red Wheel/Weiser, LLC
665 Third Street, Suite 400
San Francisco, CA 94107